LESLEY J. ROGERS holds a Personal Chair at the University
of New England, Australia. In the years since completing
a doctor of philosophy in ethology at the University of
Sussex, she has published widely in leading scientific
journals and has been author or co-author of four other
books on animal behaviour and development, including
Minds of their Own, published in 1997. Lesley's research
bridges the disciplines of neuroscience and behaviour, and
she works in both the field and the laboratory. In 1987,
the University of Sussex awarded her a Doctor of Science.

GISELA KAPLAN is an adjunct Professor at the University
of New England, Australia, and conducts research in animal
behaviour, with a disciplinary base in psychology and
ethology. She has also served as foundation professor in
social sciences at the Queensland University of Technology.
Her previous book, *Orang-utans in Borneo*, was co-written
with Lesley Rogers and was published in 1994. In addition,
she is the author of nine books and countless articles in
the social sciences. In her studies of animal behaviour,
Gisela's main areas of interest are primatology, bird
behaviour and bird song. She is a member of a voluntary
local wildlife rescue service, and raises, treats and
rehabilitates Australian native birds of prey and other avian
species.

NOT ONLY
ROARS & RITUALS

Communication in animals

Lesley J. Rogers & Gisela Kaplan

ALLEN & UNWIN

First published in 1998 by
Allen & Unwin
9 Atchison Street
St Leonards NSW 1590 Australia
Phone: (61 2) 8425 0100
Fax: (61 2) 9906 2218
E-mail: frontdesk@allen-unwin.com.au
Web: http://www.allen-unwin.com.au

National Library of Australia
Cataloguing-in-Publication entry:

Rogers, Lesley J. (Lesley Joy), 1943– .
    Not only roars & rituals: communication in animals.

    Bibliography.
    Includes index.
    ISBN 1 86448 798 4.

    1. Animal communication. 2. Animal behaviour. 3. Human–animal communication. I. Kaplan, Gisela. II. Title.

591.59

Illustrations: Tina Wilson

Set in 10/12pt Plantin by DOCUPRO, Sydney
Printed by Australian Print Group, Maryborough, Vic.

10 9 8 7 6 5 4 3 2 1

CONTENTS

LIST OF FIGURES

PREFACE

Researching animal behaviour is a humbling experience. How little we know about the hundreds of thousands of species that inhabit the globe. How little we know of the ways in which they communicate within and between species.

Constantly, we discover more about the complex capabilities of animals. One cannot help but be impressed by the wealth of social and problem-solving strategies that individual species have evolved and learnt in order to survive. From the roars and rituals that we see them performing, we begin to see meaning.

We know only too well that new knowledge of animal behaviour is needed urgently. There are many species tumbling into extinction due to our direct intervention and mistreatment of the precious legacy of the natural world. In some cases, we do not even know why these species have become endangered. In others, we know why but have found few acceptable ways of coexisting with these species. Instead, we have deprived them of the necessary life space and suitable conditions for survival. Another contributing factor towards the demise of many species is negative attitudes, fanned by ignorance. Only in this century have we truly begun to understand that the existence of animals is tied to ours and that our wellbeing depends, at least partly, on animals being allowed to maintain their lives.

In this introduction to animal communication, we

attempt to provide a sympathetic but scientifically well-founded argument about a set of complex behaviours in animals. We have endeavoured to confine the range of examples largely to mammals and birds, not because we believe in any way that the study of insects, reptiles or amphibians is less important, but because our specific focus in this book is on learning, insight and communication in species that have been studied in some detail by a range of researchers.

In our own lives, we have surrounded ourselves with animals and have gone into the field to observe animals in their natural habitat. We have had the extreme privilege of coming into close encounter with wildlife in Australia and in the rainforests of Borneo. These unusual and cherished experiences have laid the basis for this book. Behind each rare moment in which we have exchanged something deep and intangible with an animal lies an endlessly rich path to communication outside the human sphere.

LESLEY ROGERS & GISELA KAPLAN
MAY 1998

ACKNOWLEDGMENTS

Many of the ideas that formed the background of this book arose from valuable discussions of the topic with our colleagues and friends, Professors Michael Cullen, Judith Blackshaw, Richard Andrew, Peter Slater, Jeannette Ward, Dietmar Todt, Allen and the late Beatrix Gardner and also Drs Christopher Evans, Patrice Adret, Michelle Hook-Costigan and Jim Scanlan. We are also most grateful to our publisher Ian Bowring for his encouragement and assistance.

This book is dedicated to the memory of Tipsy, a dog special to us among all animals.

CHAPTER ONE

WHAT IS COMMUNICATION?

A large flock of galahs is feeding on grain scattered on newly ploughed soil. Hundreds of white crests, though flattened, are distinctly visible against the bright pink breasts and the background. Each bird maintains a characteristic social distance from the others and the hundreds of bowed yet bobbing heads suggest complete attention to feeding—until, catching sight of the approaching farmer, one bird raises its crest and screeches. At this signal of alarm the flock takes to the air as if the decision to do so were instantaneous. A signal has been sent and its meaning interpreted reliably by each member of the flock. Communication has occurred.

An enormous elephant seal lumbers up the beach, head raised, snorting as he threatens a rival. The animals make aggressive lunges at each other, blood is drawn and, with growling sounds, a truce is reached. One seal bows his head and moves away. Victor and loser have communicated on a matter of disputed territory and partner ownership has been decided.

These are grand spectacles of communication, but intimate and close-range contact has its own forms of more subtle communication. A mother orang-utan cradles her baby of seven days on her chest as she hangs by all four limbs. She smiles at the infant, as a human might do, and the infant glances up at her. A bond has formed between mother and infant and is maintained by communication.

What is communication?

Before we can explore communication in animals, it is important to have a working definition of what we mean by communication in a more general sense. There are many different definitions of communication and they vary with the field in which the researcher is working. When referring to communication in humans, psychologists often restrict the concept to acts that are performed with the *intention* of altering the behaviour of another individual. That is, the individual communicates with a purpose in mind. Linguists, however, are prepared to use a broader definition of communication to include the gestures and facial expressions that we make quite unintentionally while speaking. Given that the person receiving these signals perceives and interprets both the intentional and unintentional signals, we feel it is important to include both types of signalling in discussions of communication in humans.

There is no question that a large amount of communication among humans is intentional but there is plenty of unintentional signalling as well. For example, in many cultures, when someone gives a friendly greeting to another person, they will raise the eyebrows for a moment. This facial gesture is called 'eyebrow flashing'. Unless we make a conscious effort to think about it, we are not aware of having performed the eyebrow flash. Even the receiver may not be aware of having seen the eyebrow flash, despite the fact that it is a very important aspect of the greeting and alters the receiver's interpretation of the words spoken at the time. As Eibl-Eibesfeldt (1972) has demonstrated, greetings made without the eyebrow flash are interpreted as less friendly even though the spoken words of greeting are identical. People in some cultures do not eyebrow flash (e.g. most Japanese people do not do so) and this can create unintentional difficulties in intercultural communication. There are many other examples of what is called nonverbal communication in humans, most of which is both signalled and received unintentionally.

We can always find out what aspects of signalling by humans are intentional by asking senders exactly what message they intended to communicate. This is not possible when studying communication in animals. Even if an animal is sending a signal intentionally, it is very difficult for us to prove that this is so. The question of intentional versus unintentional signalling in animals is a hotly debated topic and one of major significance to the way in which we view and treat animals. We discuss this aspect of animal communication in Chapter Two.

We must now decide on a definition of communication that might be useful in the study of communication in animals. Communication requires one individual to send a signal of some description and another individual to receive that signal and interpret its meaning (Figure 1.1). In broad terms, we can say that an animal has signalled when it changes its behaviour, and that communication has occurred when that signal is perceived and interpreted by at least one other animal. Of course, there are many ways in which a signal can be transmitted and many ways in which it can be received.

Biologists specify how the signal must be detected and processed by the receiver: the signal must be perceived by the receiver through one or more of the sensory systems (e.g. by the sense of vision, hearing or touch). Communication is seen as a way of changing another's behaviour without the need for force or any large expenditure of energy. In a paper published in 1972, Michael Cullen, now of Monash University, illustrated this point. He said that the command 'Go jump in the lake' is a signal, whereas the push that might be delivered with it is not. The latter may, in fact, communicate something very important to the receiver, but the biologist sees this as physical force rather than true communication (Cullen 1972). In this example, the verbal command is perceived by the sense of hearing, probably in conjunction with an angry facial expression perceived by the visual system; it may change the receiver's behaviour, although, in this case, the receiver is likely to

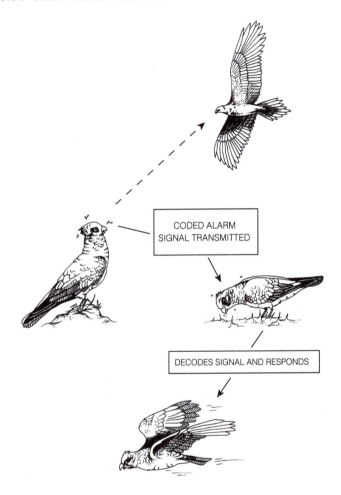

CODED ALARM
SIGNAL TRANSMITTED

DECODES SIGNAL AND RESPONDS

Figure 1.1 Sending and receiving a signal. The galah on the left has seen an eagle flying overhead and sends a coded alarm signal. This signal is transmitted through the air and it is detected by the galah on the right. The latter must discriminate and decode the message, which it does very rapidly, and then it responds by flying off. Note that the predator, too, may receive the message and respond by attacking the sender. Issuing a warning signal runs the risk of drawing attention to oneself.

take up a defensive posture rather than do what is commanded! The receiver might also choose to ignore the verbal signal, whereas that would not be possible for the physical force that follows the command.

The example of the galah giving the alarm signal is energy-efficient as a relatively small effort on the part of the galah issuing the alarm call is coupled to the large energy response of the whole flock taking flight. This signal is also time-efficient because the whole flock takes off almost instantaneously. It would be most inefficient in terms of energy and time if the signaller had to go around and physically push each member of its flock to take off. There are, however, examples of signalling that are less efficient in energy and time. Some forms of roaring or bellowing by animals require considerable energy and rather large amounts of time to signal information. Among animals we can find various degrees of economy of effort, as well as a range of signals from very obvious to very subtle.

As observers, we can tell that the signal has been perceived and interpreted only if the receiver changes its behaviour in response to the signal. Therefore, to determine whether communication has taken place we may look for a change in the sender's behaviour followed by a change in the receiver's behaviour. Sometimes, however, the receiver of the signal may decide not to respond. The decision not to respond to the signal presents a problem to human observers of animal behaviour because we have no way of knowing that communication has occurred unless the receiver responds overtly to the signal. Thus scientists who study the behaviour of animals are forced to ignore signalling that the receiver chooses to ignore; they say that communication has occurred only when the behaviour of the receiver is observed to change as a consequence of receiving the signal. Although we recognise that this approach must lead us to overlook some of the signals that pass between animals, it is not a serious problem at the present time—there is still so much that we have to learn about those signals that do, in fact, change the behaviour of the sender. It is also likely that most signals cause the receiver to respond in one way or another.

Among the scientists interested in communication between animals are behavioural ecologists, who focus on special signals that have evolved to ensure the survival of the individual animal. The warning call of the galah and its ability to trigger flight is an example of the sort of communication that interests ecologists. So too are courtship rituals that have evolved to form and maintain bonds between individuals and to ensure that mating behaviour is confined to members of the same species. Many of these involve elaborate choreography performed in a highly stylised or stereotyped manner. These signals are performed with little variation between individuals and are patterns of behaviour that are quite distinctive to the species. They are called displays. Displays are the same as signals, although usually we use the term 'displays' to refer to visual signals only, not to vocal signals or any other sensory signal.

In 1914 Julian Huxley described the extraordinary and complex mating display of the great crested grebe (*Podiceps cristatus*). The courting pair perform a complex ritual of precision swimming beginning with synchronised skimming across the surface of a lake, diving at the same time and then rising together with weeds in their beaks and assuming an upright posture by treading water while they face each other. Another is the riflebird's (*Ptiloris* sp.) rhythmic opening and closing of one wing after the other, stretching each wing over its head and bobbing the head as it does so. This visual display is accompanied by sharp rustling sounds, produced each time a wing is opened. The combined auditory and visual performance attracts the female and she responds by becoming sexually receptive. Elaborate courtship displays are performed by many species, from insects to humans.

Ethologists also study the behaviour of animals. They are interested in courtship and other displays such as these but also in somewhat less ritualised signalling that could be part of any aspect of social behaviour, unrelated to survival in any obvious way.

To study communication in animals we watch for changes in behaviour, first by the sender (or actor) of the message and then by the receiver, sometimes referred to as the 'perceiver' or the 'reactor'. Without the signal, there would be no change in the behaviour of the receiver. But it is a little more complicated than simply looking for a change in the behaviour of the sender followed by a change in the behaviour of the receiver because sometimes signals can actually *prevent* a change in the receiver's behaviour. For example, the receiver may go on performing the same behaviour as long as it is receiving a signal but switch to another behaviour only when the signal is no longer given. For example, the female riflebird may continue to show sexual responses as long as the male continues his courtship display but ceases to do so if he stops displaying. In this case, the continued presence of the signal maintains the receiver's state of readiness. We can, however, put these two types of response by the receiver together and simply say that communication has occurred when the behaviour of the receiver changes either after the signalling begins or after its stops.

Some signals are sent and received very rapidly and they cause immediate responses—the warning call is a dramatic example of this. Other signals act over a longer time frame because they are not immediately detected by the receiver. This is particularly true for signalling that uses odours. For example, marmosets, which are small monkeys of the South American rainforest, deposit scented secretions on branches; these signals are detected by other marmosets when they contact the same branches, even some time after the marmoset that deposited the message has moved away. Both short-delay and longer-delay signalling represent communication.

There is also another form of longer-delay signalling in which the signal is received and processed but the receiver's behaviour does not change until after a long period of delay.

For example, a female dog may signal that she is coming into oestrus both by her behaviour (she plays and mounts other dogs more often) and by her odour (of secretions from the vagina and in her urine). Although this signal is received by the dominant male dog in the pack, he does not respond by mating until she has reached the peak of her oestrus and is most likely to conceive. Other dogs in the pack, however, will respond by mating in the early stages of oestrus, when fertilisation is unlikely to occur. Delayed forms of signalling are more difficult to study because it is not so easy to link the sending of the signal to the receiver's change in behaviour. However, they are common among animals that attend to odours and are important aspects of communication that we humans tend to forget—we are less aware of odours, even though they do influence our behaviour.

Signals and sensory perception

Animals have a number of different senses and they make use of them all when they communicate. As humans, we are aware of the senses of vision, hearing (audition), touch (tactile sensation), taste (gustation) and smell (olfaction). We receive signals in all these sensory modalities but we are most aware of the visual and auditory ones. Language uses sound and is processed by the auditory system but, in most circumstances, it is accompanied by visual signals and sometimes tactile signals as well. We are less aware of olfactory signals and gustatory signals rarely, if ever, reach our consciousness. Other species exploit these senses to a far greater extent.

The fact that we are less conscious of communication by odours, or taste, than by audition and vision does not mean that this form of communication is absent in humans. In his book *The Scented Ape* Michael Stoddart suggests that humans might be specialists in odour communication and that it influences our behaviour much more than we think (Stoddart 1990). Like most other mammals, we have specialised glands for releasing scents and, although we are far less able to detect very low concentrations of odours (as, e.g., can dogs), we have rather excellent abilities to discriminate between odours. We may use this ability to communicate among ourselves but, if we do, much of that communication goes on unintentionally and without our conscious awareness.

Chemosignals in animals

The marmosets that deposit scents on trees do so by rubbing on the branches secretory glands located on their chests or around the genitals. These odour, or olfactory, messages are referred to as 'chemosignals'. Some chemosignals indicate the general whereabouts of a species even though the individual who deposited the scent mark may not be in the immediate vicinity at the time. Other scent marks can signal the identity of the particular species, the identity of the individual or its sex and social position. Marmosets deposit different odours that signal each of these very important social markers. All this complex information is communicated as odour, to be detected by the olfactory system.

Lemurs (*Lemur catta*) make use of scent glands on their wrists which they rub on their long, striped tails for olfactory communication. Alison Jolly, of Princeton University, has described 'stink fights' in which a number of animals gather together on the ground with their tails raised and 'throw' odours at each other by moving around and waving their tails back and forth over their heads (Jolly 1966).

The sense of olfaction is one of the major senses of many aquatic species. Eels are extremely sensitive to very low concentrations of chemicals in the water and it is thought that they use their sense of smell to return to the stream of their birth from miles away at sea. They may also use this sense to communicate with each other. A number of species of fish (e.g. minnows, catfish, sucker fish and darters) release into the water an alarm substance from specialised cells in the skin when the fish receives even minor damage. Other members of the species detect the alarm substance using the sense of smell and respond with typical fright reactions. Schooling fish, such as the minnow, aggregate and swim away from the source of the alarm substance. Other more solitary fish sink to the bottom of the water and remain motionless; others swim to the surface and may even jump out of the water. In these species the sense of olfaction is critical for survival and plays a greater role than in humans.

Electrical signals

Some species have sensory abilities that humans lack, or do not use to any known degree. The ability to sense weak electrical fields is one of these. Electric fish (Gymnotidae and Mormyridae) have organs in their tails that send out pulses of electricity (up to 300 pulses per second) and these are used for navigation and detecting prey as well as for social signalling (Bullock and Heiligenberg 1986). In some species, male and female fish pulse at different frequencies. The frequency of electrical pulses can indicate the sex of the fish and also its dominance in the social structure. Some species can vary the pulse rate to communicate. If there is a meeting between two fish sending out electrical signals at similar frequencies, either one or both will change the frequency of pulsing to avoid jamming the other's signals. Because the fish also use the electrical pulses for navigation, there would be confusion if they could not distinguish their own pulses from those of others. Dominant fish do not shift their frequency of pulsing to avoid jamming the transmission of another fish—that is up to the subordinate one.

The Australian platypus (*Ornithorhynchos anatinus*) can detect electrical signals and uses this ability to locate its prey under water. The sensory organs used for this are located around the tip of the bill and enable the platypus to detect the electrical waves produced by the contracting muscles of its prey. However, as far as we know, the platypus has no specialised organ by which it can produce electrical signals itself, and so it is unlikely that it uses electrical signalling as a means of communicating with other members of its own species. Nevertheless, a platypus could detect the electrical discharges generated when another platypus contracts its muscles during movement and could possibly exploit this as a means of communication. This has yet to be studied.

Taste

Taste is another sense that is used for communication, particularly by animals living in water. It is also used by many species of mammals, often in conjunction with olfaction. Cats, for example, deposit urine to mark territory. Other cats will approach the deposit of urine and sniff it, or even lick it or touch the upper lip on it and then lick the urine from the lip. Once on the tongue the urine can be tasted by means of receptors on the tongue and roof of the mouth. The urine contains substances characteristic of the cat from which they came and the decay of these substances also indicates how long ago the animal was in the area. By smelling and tasting the urine the receiver can also tell whether the cat is in oestrus and thus ready to mate. In other words, the taste and odour signal something about the hormonal condition of the depositing cat, and this is possible because modified products of oestrogen and testosterone are secreted into the urine.

Sheep and goats acquire similar information about the hormonal condition of the female but they taste and smell the urine by licking it from the anogenital region.

Audition

Animals also communicate by using a rich variety of auditory signals. Bird vocalisations are astounding in their variety, and most are within the hearing range of humans. Likewise, most mammals produce vocalisations that humans can hear but some species also make ultrasonic calls.

Although rats and mice are partially audible to us, most of their vocalisations are too high-pitched for us to hear. If you walk into a laboratory full of rats in cages, a range of squeals and snorts can be heard but the actual sounds are far more intense than we perceive. This cacophony of vocalisations can be revealed by recording them on a tape recorder capable of picking up ultrasound and then playing back the tape at a much slower speed so that the sounds are pitched at lower frequencies within our range of hearing.

Most rodents (rats and mice) use ultrasound to communicate. Mothers recognise their pups by the ultrasound that the pups produce and they will retrieve their pups when they make ultrasonic distress calls. Adults also communicate with each other by ultrasounds. Some primates, such as marmosets, vocalise in ultrasound, and bats specialise in it.

Certain communication sounds made by animals are quite pure in tonal quality, particularly among the songs of birds. A musical song is heard, the two most beautiful examples of which are perhaps the European nightingale (*Luscinia megarhynchos*) and the Australian magpie (*Gymnorhina tibicen*). By transcribing the sound into a visual pattern, called a sonogram or sound spectrogram, we can see what these songs look like and study them in detail (see Figure 1.2). The sound pitch, or frequency, is plotted on the vertical axis (Y axis) and time is plotted along the horizontal axis (X axis). The loudness, or intensity, of each part of the sound is indicated by the darkness of the marks plotted. A pure tone is a single frequency at any one time, although this frequency may change. Other tones have a fundamental (lowest frequency) with harmonic overtones that appear as stripes above the fundamental. The absence of overtones gives the song a characteristic pure, whistle-like quality, as illustrated by the song of the Australian pied butcherbird (*Cracticus nigrogularis*), and harmonic overtones make the song sound rich and musical (Figure 1.2). Compare this with the broad band structure of rasping calls, in which the sound energy is spread across the frequencies, and referred to as 'noise' (Figure 1.3).

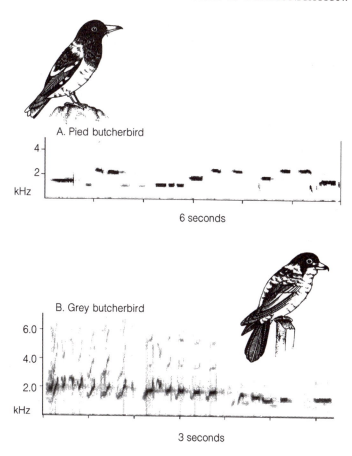

Figure 1.2 Sound spectrograms of butcherbird songs. In sound spectrograms, time is plotted on the x-axis and frequency (pitch) on the y-axis. A. The song of the pied butcherbird (*Cracticus nigrogularis*). Note the pure tones. B. The song of the grey butcher bird (*Cracticus torquatus*). Note the beginning of the song, where the syllables have louder fundamental frequencies (the dark marks at the bottom). Note also the one or two overtones above the fundamentals. The last third of the song consists of pure tones much like those of the pied butcherbird. (Sound spectrograms by G. Kaplan)

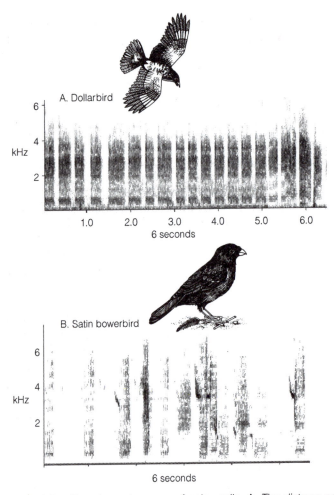

Figure 1.3 Sound spectrograms of noisy calls. A. The distress call of a dollarbird (*Eurystomus orientalis*). Note that there are some overtones but there is also a broad spread of frequencies (darkbands) called noise. B. Rasps made by a satin bowerbird (*Ptilonorhynchus violaceus*). These calls have mostly a broad band of frequencies but there are some loud tones included (black marks). In addition to the vocalisations presented here, the satin bowerbird produces a song that is very musical. (Sound spectrograms by G. Kaplan)

Despite the fact that noisy birds do exist and that even songbirds produce some noisy calls, many bird-songs have tonality (musical sounds). By comparison, many vocalisations produced by mammals are noisy, although there are many exceptions, such as the calls of gibbons and certain calls made by squirrel monkeys, macaque monkeys and even chimpanzees. We give further examples in the chapters to follow.

Vision

Communication using the sense of vision is widespread among species. These signals are made by moving limbs in certain ways (gesturing), by adopting certain body postures or by making facial expressions. The baboon that bares its teeth is not smiling but signalling its state of anger. A dog indicates submission by arching its back and lowering its tail, sometimes wrapping the tail between its hind legs. A lizard that bobs its head up and down is either signalling ownership of territory or performing a courtship ritual. There are many examples of visual signalling in animals and we mention more in the pages to follow. On some occasions visual signals are used alone, while at other times they occur in conjunction with vocalisations or communication signals involving the other senses. Combined signalling using more than one sense may ensure that the receiver 'gets the right message'.

Choosing the best signal

To make sure that a signal can be detected by the receiver it is important to choose the best form of signalling for each particular environment.

Signalling over a 'noisy' background

When the famous musician Paganini played with an orchestra he made sure that the sounds of his violin would be heard above the orchestra by tuning it a quarter of a tone higher than the other instruments. This sharpening of pitch was not enough for his playing to sound out of tune but it allowed his notes to penetrate above the background harmony of the orchestra. This technique is exploited by some animals that need to signal over loud background noise. There is an insect in the rainforests of South East Asia that we call 'the chainsaw insect' because its penetrating whine is heard above the cacophony of other insects as a sharp, higher frequency.

Being seen as well as heard is a special problem in forests because only certain visual signals will be seen easily in the dappled and varying light of dense forest and against the background of complex patterns formed by vines, trunks and leaves. If you wanted to send a visual signal in a 'noisy' visual environment, it would be pointless to display stripes or patches of black and white. Zebras are actually camouflaged by their black and white stripes when they stand still in dappled light beside or under bushes. Black and white patterning makes effective camouflage, but the receiver would be unlikely to detect a signal that depended on the use of such patterns unless it involved movements that made the patterns more visible. It is not surprising therefore that many species of the forest are brightly coloured on those parts of their bodies that are used to send visual signals.

At dawn and dusk

At dawn and dusk the light is purplish and animals that forage for their food at these times are better able to avoid predators if their colouration blends in with a background illuminated by purplish light, made up of the longer (red) wavelengths together with the shorter (blue and violet) wavelengths. The middle-of-the-range (yellow and green) wavelengths are missing in purple light and so animals with these colours would appear dark. This means that the best way to signal in these conditions would be to use blue, red or purple for brightness and yellow or green for contrast.

Galahs are most active at dawn and dusk and at these times, when they tend to feed on the ground, their grey backs provide camouflage from aerial predators. Flocks of galahs are also quite difficult to see against the evening or dawn sky until the flock turns suddenly and there is a bright flash of the rose-coloured breasts, a sight never forgotten. It may be some form of social signal to do with group cohesion but that is not known.

In the rainforest

The daytime quality of light in forests varies with the density of the vegetation, the angle of the sun and the amount of cloud in the sky, as shown in detail by John Endler, formerly of the University of California and now at James Cook University in Australia (Endler 1993). Both animals and plants have different appearances in these various lighting conditions. A colour or pattern that is relatively indistinct in one kind of light may be quite conspicuous in another.

In the varied and constantly changing light environment of the forest, an animal must be able to send visual signals to members of its own species and at the same time avoid being detected by predators. Hiding from predators may be achieved by choosing the light environment in which its pattern is least visible. This may require moving to different parts of the forest at different times of the day or under different weather conditions, or it may be achieved by changing colour according to the changing light conditions. Many species of amphibia (frogs and toads) and reptiles (lizards and snakes) are able to change their colour patterns for camouflage. Some also signal by changing their colour. The chameleon lizard has the most striking ability to do this. Some chameleon species can change from a rather dull appearance to a full riot of carnival colours in seconds. By this means they signal their level of aggression or readiness to mate.

Other species take into account the changing conditions

of light by performing their visual displays only when the light is right. A bird of paradise may put himself in the limelight by displaying his spectacular plumage in the best stage-setting to attract a female. Certain butterflies move into spots of sunlight that have penetrated to the forest floor and display by opening and closing their beautifully patterned wings in the bright spotlights. They also compete with each other for the best spot of sunlight.

Very little light filters through the canopy of leaves and branches to reach ground level, or close to the ground, and here the yellow to green wavelengths predominate. A signal might be most easily seen if it is maximally bright. In the green to yellow lighting conditions of the lowest levels of the forest, yellow and green would be the brightest colours but, when signalling, these colours would not be very visible if the animal were sitting on a yellowish to greenish background. As John Endler explains, the best signal depends not only on its brightness but also on how well it contrasts with the background against which it must be seen (Endler 1993). The green tree frogs that inhabit Australia's rainforests (15 different species of *Litoria*) are coloured in shades of green on their backs and bright yellow or white on the under-surfaces of their bodies and limbs. These colours may provide camouflage in the lower levels of the rainforest. Colours close to, but not identical to, yellow and green are best for signalling in this locality because they are bright and can also be distinguished from the background. In this part of the forest, therefore, red and orange are the best colours to choose for signalling and this is exactly the signal choice of the ground-walking Australian brush turkey (*Alectura lathami*). This species, which lives in the rainforests and scrub lands of the east coast of Australia, has a brown to black plumage with bare bright red skin on the head and neck and a neck collar of orange-yellow, loosely hanging skin. During courtship and aggressive displays, the coloured neck collar is enlarged by inflating sacs in the neck region, and the turkey flings about a pendulous part of the coloured signalling apparatus as it utters calls designed to attract or repel. This impressive display is clearly visible in the light spectrum illuminating the forest floor.

In higher realms of the forest or in more open areas where trees have been felled, blue-grey illumination is predominant and here blue or blue-green colouration is the brightest and again red or orange provides the best contrast. The blue-green and red combination of colours is exploited by the swift parrot (*Lathamus discolor*), which inhabits open forest in south eastern Australia, and the eclectus parrot, (*Eclectus roratorus*) in the upper levels of tropical rainforests and adjacent eucalypt woodlands of the most northerly tip of Queensland. Interestingly, the best signal colours are sported differently by the male and female eclectus parrots. The male is bright green with scarlet red flanks under the wings and a large orange-red beak, while the female is bright blue and scarlet red with a black beak. The male has blue feathers in the wings but these are displayed only in flight.

Species that seek out small gaps in the canopy, where reddish light predominates, should signal with red, orange or yellow for maximum brightness and use purple or blue for contrast. The male Australian rainbow lorikeet (*Trichoglossus haematodus*) uses this combination of colours in clownish fashion: it has a blue to purplish head and underbelly, a bright red beak and an orange and red breast together with a green back and green upper surface of the wings. The green upper surface provides camouflage despite the conspicuous garb used for signalling because it disrupts the outline of the bird's shape; in particular, the green upper surface conceals the bird from aerial predators such as falcons or hawks. This species is a striking example of the outcome of evolutionary processes that have selected for a balance between colours that will conceal and colours that can be used to signal.

Less colourful birds and other species that inhabit the rainforest tend to rely on forms of signalling other than visual, particularly over longer distances. The hooting calls of the rhinoceros hornbill characterise the South East Asian rainforest, as do the unmistakable calls of the gibbons. There is also the long, rather terrifying call of the male orang-utan that carries over considerable distances to advertise his presence. In densely wooded environments, sound is the best means of communication over distance because, in comparison with light, it travels with little impediment from trees and other vegetation. In forests, visual signals can be seen only at shorter distances when not obstructed by trees. The male riflebird exploits both these modes of signalling simultaneously in his courtship display. The sounds made as each wing is opened carry extremely well over distance and advertise his presence widely. The ritualised visual display communicates in close quarters when the female has approached.

Under the sea

Under the sea, too, light conditions are varied and constantly changing. As snorkelers will know, shallow areas of the sea have ever-changing patterns of light of different wavelengths and intensity. To be able to change colour, as many sea creatures can, is a distinct advantage here—it can be used to avoid being seen by predators. In this environment, too, social signalling commonly involves changing colour. The cuttlefish not only changes colour to camouflage itself against the background but also flashes colour messages to other members of its own species, sometimes changing colour only on the side of the body that its conspecific (member of same species) will see as it swims past. The other side retains its camouflage pattern. This is an extreme case of directing the signal in precisely the desired direction, at the same time avoiding detection by other cuttlefish and predators.

As we have seen, sound signals too must be chosen according to the auditory environment. Sound can be heard over greater distances in certain conditions. For example, sound travels well in water and this is why whales use sound to signal over many miles. Sound is attenuated by vegetation and the surface of the sea-floor. In general, high-pitched sounds are attenuated more than deep, low-pitched ones. So calls that need to advertise the presence of the sender over long distances should be both loud and deep, like those used by whales. The same principles apply to sounds transmitted in air and thus the long call of the orang-utan and the bellow of the elephant are both loud and low-pitched.

We have seen that olfaction is an important sense in fish communication. Although fish use visual and auditory signals as well, chemicals released into the water may be carried by currents over very long distances. They are ideal for long-distance communication under water, although the direction of current flow limits the signal to downstream receivers. The males of some species of fish signal their presence to females by releasing chemicals into the water. When females detect the chemical signal, using their olfactory sense, they swim upstream towards the male. Once the male comes into sight, visual signals play an additional role in beckoning the female.

In the dark

Visual signals are ineffective in dark environments such as caves or burrows. Thus species living in these environments communicate by sounds or smells. Bats use ultrasound, sound of such high frequency (or pitch) that it is outside the hearing range of humans. They use ultrasound both to navigate in the dark and to communicate with each other. Cave-dwelling oil birds (*Steatornis caripensis*) and swiftlets (*Collocalia* sp.) also use ultrasound to navigate and communicate when they are inside the dark caves where they nest, although they use vision outside the cave.

In their underground burrows, moles and rats may communicate by sound. In fact, vision is so unimportant in this environment that one burrowing species, the mole-rat (*Spadix ehrenbergi*), has effectively no eyes. Through the course of time and the process of evolution, the eyes have become minuscule in size and the skin and fur have grown over them. Even the external ears are not detectible. The mole-rat has become a cylindrical-shaped animal with short legs and tail, the perfect design for moving along tunnels only just big enough for it. These animals communicate with each other by tapping their snouts on the walls of the burrow. The vibrations are seismic signals that can be detected by a mole-rat in another tunnel of the burrow even at quite a distance away. At closer quarters the mole-rats communicate by vocalising rather than tapping, and they also use odours. A recent study by Uri Shanas and Joseph Terkel (1997), of Tel Aviv University, has demonstrated that mole-rats release an odorous secretion from a gland in the orbit of the eye when they groom themselves. The secretion runs down a duct and out through the nostrils. By grooming, the mole-rats spread the secretion over their bodies and it serves to decrease aggression between males. In effect, the odour signals 'Don't fight'.

Communication by seismic vibrations is also common in nocturnal desert rodents. North American kangaroo rats (*Dipodomys*) and African gerbils (a type of rat, including *Gerbillus* and other genera) strike their feet against the ground to produce drumrolls that characterise the individual's species. Jan Randall, of San Francisco State University, has shown that kangaroo rats have individual signature rhythms that communicate the animal's identity and lower the risk of disputes over territory among neighbours (Randall 1997).

The white-lipped frog of Puerto Rico (*Leptodactylus albilabris*) is believed to have the greatest sensitivity to seismic stimuli of all known species. It embeds itself in mud and produces advertisement chirps or aggressive chuckles; as it expands its vocal sac in order to make these calls, the sac strikes against the muddy substrate to produce a seismic 'thump' that is detected by other members of its species in the vicinity.

In addition to the effective use of sound and odour to

communicate in the dark, electrical signals may be used. Electrical signals are an effective mode of communication in the murky waters of streams and this is how the electric fish of South and Middle America navigate and signal to each other. We have already seen the way in which electric fish communicate their sex and dominance.

Measuring communication in animals

It is not always simple to prove that communication has occurred and it is even more difficult to decipher exactly what has been communicated. First we need to know a lot about the behaviour of the species we are investigating, and then we have to use certain techniques to determine whether a signal has been sent and received. We may detect that communication has occurred by observing behaviour to see whether a particular activity performed by one animal consistently leads to a change in the behaviour of another animal, or animals. This requires very careful observation and must be repeated many times. Once the initial observations have been made, they can be followed up by experiments designed to determine the exact nature of the communication. There are several clever ways of doing this.

Audio playback experiments

One of the main ways to study communication in animals is to record the signal of interest and then play it back to the animals and see whether they respond in a predictable way. For example, many songbirds sing to advertise their territory. These territorial songs can be recorded on audiotape and then played back over and over again through a loudspeaker placed in an unoccupied territory. If males of the species stay out of the area where the loudspeaker is located, it may be concluded that the song is indeed a territorial vocalisation. Of course, it is not as simple as this because we need to have an experimental control. We need to know how rapidly males would move into an unoccupied territory without a loudspeaker broadcasting the song.

Experiments of this type have demonstrated that the European great tit (*Parus major*) produces a specific territorial song. John Krebs, of Oxford University, removed pairs of great tits from their territories in a forest and then placed a loudspeaker broadcasting the song of the great tits in some of the territories and left other territories empty. He found that the territories without loudspeakers were reoccupied far sooner than those with the loudspeakers broadcasting the song (Krebs 1977). This shows that the song does advertise that a given territory is taken and warns other males of the species to stay out of it. However, the fact that the territories with loudspeakers were eventually occupied suggests that continued maintenance of a territory requires more than simply singing in one spot. It might require moving around in the territory and using visual displays to accompany the song.

While this particular experimental procedure can demonstrate that a song advertises territory and signals to other males to keep out, it is important to go a step further to see how specific the song has to be in order to communicate this signal effectively. This can be done by playing another song, or a modified version of the song, through loudspeakers placed in unoccupied territories to see whether these sounds also inhibit males of the species from moving in to occupy the territory. If they do not keep males out of the territory, or if they are clearly less effective in doing so than the original song, we can conclude that there is some specificity in the song. If, on the other hand, sounds other than the song also keep males out of the area around the speaker, there would be no such specificity and we would be unable to conclude that the song itself was communicating territory ownership.

Using this technique, it is possible to determine exactly what aspects of the song convey the important information about territory ownership. This can be done by modifying the recorded song in various ways. Parts of it might be left out, or the song played backwards. Alternatively, the order or sequence of the syllables (parts of the song; see Figure 1.2) may be changed. There are many ways of modifying the song. The effect of playing back the modified song can then be compared with the effect of playing back the unmodified song. In this manner, it is possible to single out the essential aspects of the song that warn other males to keep out of the territory.

John Krebs followed up his first experiment by playing back modified songs. In fact, he noticed that the great tits have repertoires of songs. One male may sing up to eight different types of song. As individual birds vary in how many song types they sing, he was interested to see whether the size of the repertoire would alter the signal, making it more or less effective. To do this, he located loudspeakers that played back only one song in some unoccupied territories and speakers that played back repertoires of up to eight songs in other territories. The territories in which the larger repertoire was broadcast were reoccupied after a much longer delay than those in which the smaller repertoire was played (Krebs et al. 1978). This demonstrated that singing more song types together in a repertoire is a more effective signal than singing only one song type. Hence males with more elaborate songs can maintain their territory more effectively than those with less elaborate ones.

The fact that variations of a song produce different results raises another issue about the design of playback experiments, as first realised by Donald Kroodsma, of the University of Massachusetts (Kroodsma 1990). It is important to select many different songs to play back. In some of the earlier playback experiments, only one song, or very few songs, were played through the loudspeaker and this could have seriously limited the results. In fact, many avian species learn to recognise the territorial songs of other members of their species holding territories beside their own and respond differently to the territorial calls of their neighbours compared with those of birds from more distant territories.

Emma Brindley, of the University of Nottingham, has investigated the responses of European robins (*Erithacus rubecula*) to the songs of neighbours versus strangers (Brindley 1991). Despite the large and complex song repertoire of the European robins, they were able to discriminate between the songs of neighbours and strangers. When they heard the tape recording of the stranger, they began to sing sooner, sang more songs and overlapped their songs with the playback more often than they did on hearing a neighbour's song. As Brindley suggests, the overlapping of song may be an aggressive response. However, this difference in responding to neighbour versus stranger occurred only when the neighbour's song was played by a loudspeaker placed at the boundary between that particular neighbour's territory and the territory of the bird being tested. If the same neighbour's song was played at another boundary, one separating the territory of the test subject from another neighbour, it was treated as the call of a stranger. Not only does this result demonstrate that the robins associate locality with familiar songs, but it also shows that the choice of songs used in playback experiments is highly important.

The playback technique can be used to study the territorial vocalisations of other species. It can also be used to study other kinds of auditory signals. For example, Jan Randall determined the meaning of the drumrolls made by kangaroo rats (mentioned earlier) by playing back foot-drumming recordings of three different species to wild populations of each species. Two of the species (*Dipodomys spectabilis* and *D. ingens*) responded to hearing the playback by drumming and the other species (*D. desertii*) approached the loudspeaker. These responses to the playback are typical of each species—*D. desertii* chases intruders away and only rarely drums the feet, whereas the other two species engage in drumming exchanges. Thus, each species responds to hearing the playback of sounds used in communicating about identity and territory in ways typical of the species.

The playback technique can be used to investigate other forms of communication, not just those about territory. For example, playing the songs of male canaries to female canaries stimulates them to build nests. Alternatively, playing the warning call of a species stimulates appropriate evasive action. Christopher Evans and Peter Marler (1993), at the University of California in Davis, found that the alarm call of cockerels differs depending on whether they see a predator on the ground or in the air. When they see a hawk, or even a hawk-like image, moving overhead, they emit a long screech (Figure 1.4A), which is entirely different from the call given when they see a predator on the ground, such as a dog or raccoon (Figure 1.4B). The latter is a repeated pattern of short pulses ending with a little flourish. It should be noted that the warning call signalling the presence of an aerial predator is a thin high-pitched sound, as is the warning call of the galah and many other species. The source of such calls is difficult to locate and hence the caller is less likely to be detected by an aerial predator.

Having recorded these two calls made by the cockerels, Evans and Marler used the playback technique to assess whether the calls signalled anything specific to other chickens. They tested each chicken individually in a cage in the laboratory, where it could not see any predators and was not exposed to any other changing visual stimulus that might cause it to vocalise. They then played the two kinds of alarm signals through a loudspeaker. When the aerial alarm call was played back, a chicken hearing it would crouch and look up as if trying to catch sight of the predator in the air. When the ground-predator alarm call was played, the chicken hearing it would run for cover or strut while calling in a way that might drive the predator away. Thus, the two alarm calls have specificity and signal to the receiver to take the appropriate measures to avoid being caught.

Vervet monkeys (*Cercopithecus aethiops*) also produce different vocalisations for different predators. Males make a deep barking call for a leopard and females make short, high-pitched chirps in the same circumstance. A chutter-like

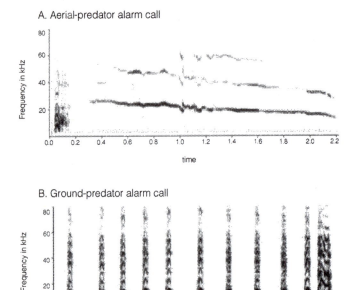

Figure 1.4 Sound spectrograms of alarm calls of chickens. Different calls are produced to signal the presence of predators on the ground or in the air. A. The alarm call given when an aerial predator (hawk) is seen flying overhead. B. The alarm call given when a ground predator (dog or raccoon) is seen. (Adaptations of recordings made by C.S. Evans and P. Marler; sound spectrogram courtesy of C.S. Evans)

call is made for a snake and a single cough-like call for an eagle. Dorothy Cheney and Robert Seyfarth carried out playback experiments at the field site for their research in Africa. They found that the vervet monkeys took the appropriate evasive action for the predator indicated by the call (Cheney & Seyfarth 1990; Seyfarth et al. 1980). When the leopard call was played, they would dash to the nearest tree and climb it. On hearing the snake call, the monkeys would stand up on their hind limbs and peer into the grass. When the eagle call was played, they would look up and take cover, not dissimilar to the evasive action taken by the chicken on hearing its own aerial alarm call.

Living in the same territory as the vervet monkeys are starlings (superb starlings) and these birds also make different calls for eagles and terrestrial predators. Cheney and Seyfarth discovered that the vervet monkeys knew the meaning of the predator calls made by the starlings as well as their own species-specific calls. When the starling's eagle alarm call was played over a loudspeaker, the monkeys looked up; when the starling's ground-predator alarm call was played, most of the monkeys ran to the trees. No response was given when the starling's song was played back, and that was a control for the experiment because the song does not indicate the presence of any predator. It would seem that the monkeys have learnt to interpret the alarm signals of the starling. In this way different species living in the same area may make use of each other's communication signals.

Video playback experiments

Auditory signals have so far been the main focus of attention in the playback technique, but recent advances in video imaging have made the technique applicable to visual signals. It is now possible to make video recordings easily and, by use of digital manipulation, to change the recorded image for playback. Thus the behaviour thought to be a visual signal can be video recorded and played back to another member of the species in a controlled setting to see whether it elicits a reliable response in the receiver. Then, just as for playback of altered song, components of the video image can be eliminated or modified to determine exactly what aspects of the image are essential for the signal.

Of course, this technique will be successful only if the species being studied pays attention to video images, which are two-dimensional and flicker. Humans cannot see flicker when it is very fast but some animals can see flicker at frequencies which we cannot. Fluorescent lights flicker on and off at so fast a rate that we perceive the light as being on continuously. However, some birds may be able to see the flicker and it would appear to them as a strobe light does to us. Video playback may also be seen to flicker by some species and this would make it far from suitable for testing those species.

Nevertheless, Evans and Marler found that chickens do attend to video images in experiments where they used the video image of a chicken as a companion to a rooster stimulated to give alarm calls. First, they had found that a rooster is much more likely to emit an alarm call on seeing an aerial predator when another live chicken is present in an adjoining cage. Next, they were able to show that replay of a video image of a chicken, with accompanying sound-track, would replace the live chicken and have the same effect of enhancing alarm calling by the rooster. Then they played a video image of another species, a bobwhite quail, and found it to be less effective than the video image of the rooster's own species (Evans & Marler 1991).

Video imaging has also been used to study the visual signals made by male lizards (*Anolis*) in courtship and aggressive encounters. Joseph Macedonia and Christopher Evans, formerly of the Animal Communication Laboratory at the University of California and now at Macquarie University in Australia, and Jonathan Losos, of the Department of Biology at Washington University, used video playback to investigate head-bobbing and pulsing of the dewlap, the skin under the chin that can be extended and contracted, performed by two species of *Anolis* when males encounter each other. These are aggressive visual displays. The researchers found that the video images of head-bobbing and dewlap displays elicited similar displays by the live lizards watching them, and that seeing a video of a member of the same species was more effective in eliciting the aggressive display than seeing a video of another species.

This illustrates at least some degree of species specificity in visual signals of aggression (Macedonia et al. 1994).

Video recording and playback can also be used to study communication by facial expression in animals. The image can be varied by changing the eyes, nose, mouth or other features, either by distorting its contribution to the total facial expression or by eliminating each feature in turn from the expression. In this manner, the relative importance of the various features in any particular facial expression can be determined. For example, orang-utans, and many other primates, perform one kind of play-threat display by opening the mouth, puffing up the lips, showing the teeth and raising the eyebrows (Figure 1.5). It is not known which (if not all) of these features signals to another orang-utan, but now it would be possible to find out by using video playback of manipulated images.

Playing video images to animals to study signalling has the advantage of being able to repeat exactly the same sequence of videotaped recordings as many times as the experimenter wishes. Exactly the same sequence can be presented to different animals, or again and again to the same animal, thus testing the reliability of the signal.

Communication within and between species

Most communication occurs between members of the same species (intraspecies communication) but there are occasions when one species signals to another or when one species responds to the signals of another species (interspecies communication). We have seen one example of the latter: the response of vervet monkeys to the eagle alarm call of starlings living in the same area. In this case, it is most unlikely that the starling is directing its signal to the vervet monkeys, but rather to other members of its own species. The monkeys are simply able to 'tune in' to the starlings' signals and exploit them.

There are, however, examples of an individual of one species signalling directly to an individual of another species.

Figure 1.5   Open mouth play-threat display of an orang-utan. Note the puffed area around the mouth, bared teeth and raised eyebrows. This signal was directed towards another orang-utan and it was followed by a play-attack of that orang-utan. (Photograph by G. Kaplan)

This is often seen in prey–predator interactions. When cornered by a predator, the last resort of the prey is to attempt to scare off the predator by looking as big as possible, showing bright colours and making a terrifying sound. Toads adopt a threat posture in which they puff up with air and stand high on their paws, thereby making themselves look as large as they can.

Other strategies can be used when cornered. The sudden flash of a brightly coloured signal may confuse the predator just long enough for the prey to get away. This tactic is used by some lizards (e.g. *Anolis*) which perform push-ups and flash the dewlap when they encounter a predator such as a snake (Leal & Rodriguez 1997). The Australian frill-necked lizard has an even more impressive display to communicate with a predator: it raises the large ruff around its neck so that, from face on, it looks many times larger; it opens its mouth to reveal the brightly coloured tongue and lining of the mouth and hisses. This striking display is usually followed by a rapid retreat, running on hind limbs, ruff still raised. If the predator has been thrown momentarily off guard by the display, the prey may have a slight advantage as it beats its retreat.

Another form of interspecies signalling by prey to predator is aimed at deflecting the attack to a less vulnerable part of the prey's body. The eye-like patterns (ocelli) on the wings of some moths and butterflies may be used in this way, as first demonstrated by David Blest (1957). When a bird is poised to attack, the moth or butterfly opens its wings to reveal the ocelli. As birds are very interested in eyes, they tend to peck at the ocelli instead of the body of the moth or butterfly itself. Alternatively, revealing the ocelli may startle the bird and give the prey time to escape. This form of interspecies communication is so important for survival that some species have stylised the display by using different ways of flashing the ocelli, either rhythmically or in a more static fashion.

Plovers feign injury to deflect the attention of the predator away from their offspring in the nest on the ground. As the predator approaches, the plover moves away from the nest in a manner that would signal she has a broken wing. This is a dramatic form of interspecies signalling. Another form of prey-to-predator signalling has been termed pursuit-deterrent signalling. Tim Caro, of the University of California at Davis, has used the term 'pursuit-deterrent signalling' for communication in which the prey signals that it has seen the predator or that it is able to escape (Caro 1995). The effect of the signal appears to be to stop the predator from attacking. For example, on seeing a predator, the Thomson's gazelle performs stotting (high leaps from all fours with the tail up displaying the white rump), bannertail kangaroo rats drum their feet and swamp wrens flick their tails.

In fact, the rich variety of signals between prey and predator is a manifestation of the importance of communication in survival. Social relationships within species are established, maintained and terminated by communication. Communication between species may be of mutual benefit or aimed at enhancing the survival of the signaller over that of the receiver. Usually, however, the outcome of signalling is exclusively in the interests of the sender rather than the receiver. Even though prey–predator signalling may lead the predator to abandon its pursuit, this may be in the predator's interest because success is more likely to be achieved by stalking a prey that has not seen the predator.

Conclusion

The terms 'communication' and 'signalling' are really quite interchangeable. Animals indulge in a great deal of communication about a wide range of matters. Their social life depends on communication. Communication occurs in even the simplest organisms that interact with each other, even if it is only to mate. In higher species, a rich variety of communication occurs, making use of all the sensory systems and ranging from simple signals to complex stylised displays. Different species use the different sensory systems to varying extents, depending on where they live and the most effective way to send a signal. We may say that communication is entirely context-dependent, meaning that what is communicated and when communication occurs depends on the environmental context surrounding the animal.

As observers of animals, we must first establish whether communication has actually occurred by determining whether a signal sent by one animal changes the behaviour of the animal receiving it. Then we must determine exactly what has been signalled. Most communication between animals must depend on the use of specific signals that will not be ambiguous, but there are examples of the same signal being used in entirely different contexts and causing quite different responses by the receiver. These signals would seem to be less specific, unless the same signal means something different when it is given in a different context, or the signals are, in fact, different in subtle ways that have eluded us. By using the playback technique and modifying the calls played back, we should eventually be able to distinguish between these alternatives.

There is enormous diversity in the signals that different species use. Walking through the rainforest, swimming on a coral reef or simply sitting in the garden, we become aware of the many signals that are being sent and received between animals, so few of which we understand.

CHAPTER TWO

SIGNALLING: INTENTIONAL OR UNINTENTIONAL

Humans do not always communicate verbally. Sometimes we communicate vocally, using sounds that are not words, and sometimes by touching another person. In particular, whether we are speaking or not, we make facial expressions. These forms of communication are all referred to as 'nonverbal' communication. Nonverbal communication may be intentional or unintentional. In fact, a large amount of the communication that we make by nonverbal utterances or facial expressions is unintentional, signalling something about our internal (emotional) state.

The fact that there are many different vocalisations that humans emit without any intention of communicating raises the possibility that vocalisations made by animals are also utterances made unintentionally. Many people believe that all forms of signalling by animals are unintentional. Those who take this view make an absolute division between animals and humans, reserving intentional communication for humans alone. They believe that animals simply emit vocalisations, and other signals, unthinkingly. They assume that the vocalisations and other signals made by animals are involuntary, meaning that they cannot be controlled consciously and are simply generated as an automatic statement of the animal's emotional state.

For example, a chick that peeps when it is cold and twitters when it finds a warm place does so as if it were a little machine, not because it actually wants to communicate that it feels distress or pleasure. In fact, some people widen the divide between animals and humans even further by assuming that animals may not actually be aware of feeling distress, pleasure or any other internal state. The animal is seen as a robot without feelings or the ability to think, let alone communicate intentionally.

This view of animals has an equally mechanistic explanation of the animal that receives and responds to the signal. The hen might respond to the chick's distress calls by leading it to food but she does so without thinking, not knowing what she has heard or even that she is responding. The interaction between the chick and the hen is interpreted as simply one little robot making a sound that causes a slightly larger robot to change its behaviour. This is an extreme position but it is a view that is expressed in different forms and to various degrees in the scientific literature on animals and, even more often, in the anthropological literature dealing with the evolution of what are considered to be uniquely human attributes.

To refute this attitude to animals we would need to consider whether animals are capable of thinking for themselves and whether they can actually feel things that they communicate to others. It is not our intention to explore the broad topic of thinking and awareness in animals here (see *Minds of their Own* by Lesley Rogers 1997) but we do consider those aspects of communication that tell us something about whether or not animals communicate intentionally.

The fact that a signal is sent and leads to a change in the behaviour of another animal is not, in itself, evidence that the sender intended to communicate or that the receiver intended to respond. It is very difficult to prove that the animal sending the signal intends to communicate but there is new evidence showing that animals communicate specific information in specific circumstances. These findings work against the notion that animals emit signals simply as a reflection of their emotional state and in an uncontrolled and random way. Emotions certainly play a role in signalling by animals, as they do in humans, but communication in animals is not simply an automatic statement of the emotions, as we discuss below (see also Marler & Evans 1996).

The effect of having an audience

If an animal communicates unintentionally it should signal in exactly the same way whether it happens to be alone or in the company of other animals; if it communicates intentionally, we might expect it to confine its signalling to occasions when it has an audience.

Warning calls are a special case for considering the presence or absence of an audience. Let us consider the case of a chicken (*Gallus gallus*) that emits a warning call when it catches sight of a hawk flying overhead. In Chapter One, we saw that cockerels make one warning call for a predator seen flying overhead and a different call for one approaching on the ground (the aerial-predator versus the ground-predator alarm call: Figure 1.4). Thus, a cockerel makes a specific screeching call when he sees the aerial predator but, by doing so, he draws attention to himself and increases the chance that he will be taken by the predator. By issuing the warning call, the individual may save the group but risks his own life.

There has been much debate about whether this is a genuinely altruistic act on the part of the caller or whether it is not particularly altruistic because the individual shares some of his genes with other members of the flock and, therefore, by calling he enhances the survival of those genes. It is not our intention to enter this debate here, but it is our concern to consider whether the individual issuing the warning call does so intentionally or simply emits the vocalisation when his internal state is changed by seeing the predator.

Obviously, the bird that sees the predator feels fear. The call made could simply be an expression of that internal state of fear (i.e. an automatic, unintentional signal of emotional state). The first piece of evidence to indicate that this is not the case is the fact that different calls are made for aerial and ground predators although both predators induce a state of fear. It could, however, be suggested that an aerial predator elicits more fear than a ground predator (or vice versa) and that the different calls are merely a reflection of the amount of fear that the individual feels. Switching from one call to another completely different call as the internal state of fear increases does appear to occur in some species (see later in this chapter). In other species, however, increasing states of arousal (fear) are accompanied by the same call being made more often or more loudly.

The second piece of evidence against the idea that the two different alarm calls are made unintentionally is the fact that the presence or absence of an audience influences whether calling occurs or not. If the cockerel happened to be alone when he saw the predator, there would be no advantage in making a warning call. In fact, to issue a warning in this circumstance would be nothing less than disadvantageous. However, if the cockerel cannot control his vocalisations and merely emits the warning call as a reflection of his particular internal state at the time, he will call irrespective of whether he is alone or in the presence of other members of his species. On the other hand, if the cockerel can control his vocalisations and raises the alarm only when he has the intention of warning other chickens, he should not call when alone.

The latter is the case, as Peter Marler and colleagues at the University of California in Davis have shown. They measured the alarm calls made by a cockerel in a cage with a video monitor placed overhead. When an image of a hawk in flight, or an approximation to one, was presented on the video monitor the cockerel made aerial-alarm calls but only when there was a male or female of his own species in a nearby cage (Karakashian et al. 1988). He rarely uttered an alarm call when the same cage was empty or when it contained a bird from a related but different species (they used a bobwhite quail). An audience of the cockerel's own species had to be present for alarm calling to occur. As we saw in Chapter One, Marler and Evans were later able to show that a video image of a hen of the same species would also serve as an audience instead of a live chicken.

The need for an audience before aerial-alarm calling will occur shows that the cockerel is not a simple robot emitting alarm calls when he is triggered by the appropriate stimulus (the predator). The social environment is taken into account before calling occurs. It could be said that the cockerel does not call when alone because he does not become sufficiently aroused by seeing the hawk unless another chicken is present. This could mean that he does not call intentionally but requires two conditions to be met before he will call automatically. Such an explanation will suit those who wish to make an absolute distinction between the communication systems of animals and humans. However, it does not seem to be correct because the cockerels showed the same amount of looking overhead, crouching, immobility, scuttling away and sleeking down of their feathers with and without an audience. Apart from the absence of alarm calling, the cockerels when alone reacted to the hawk to the same extent, irrespective of the presence or absence of the hen (Marler & Evans 1996). This shows that they were, in fact, just as afraid when alone as when they had an audience. We may, therefore, conclude that the cockerel actively suppresses alarm calling when alone. We think the most likely interpretation of these findings is that the cockerel makes the warning call only when there is a reason for doing so and that, when he does call, he does so with the intention of warning other members of his own species. More experiments will be necessary before we can be sure of this explanation.

We have outlined just one example so far. We saw in Chapter One that vervet monkeys give different alarm calls for different predators. The presence of an audience also determines whether alarm calls will be given. Solitary vervet monkeys have been observed to escape from an approaching leopard in total silence. Apparently, the absence of other vervet monkeys negated the need to call and alarm calling was suppressed, just as with the cockerel.

Cheney and Seyfarth (1985, 1990) also conducted experiments on captive vervet monkeys, demonstrating that adult females give more alarm calls when their offspring are present. Despite this effect of audience, however, Cheney and Seyfarth conclude that vervet monkeys do not really know anything about the mind-state of their audience (i.e. whether their audience knows or does not know that a predator is nearby). The researchers base this conclusion on the fact that the monkeys go on making alarm calls long after every other monkey in the group has seen the predator; and, in the presence of their offspring, mothers call no more often, or differently, for predators that offer great threat to their offspring than for those of lesser threat.

Although these observations suggest that the signaller does not differentiate its own vulnerability from that of its audience, more information is needed before a firm conclusion can be reached about the ability of the monkeys to modulate calling according to the state of knowledge of group members. However, it is clear that they can vary alarm calling according to the presence or absence of an audience. As more such details about the complexity of communication in animals are being revealed, it becomes more certain that animals can control when they signal, by vocal or other means, and also what signal they will use in a given context. They do not signal impulsively and involuntarily.

The presence of an audience also increases the calls that cockerels produce in the presence of food (Evans & Marler 1994). There is a typical food call, consisting of repeated pulses of sound, that the cockerel produces when he sees food, or another stimulus that he associates with food, and this call attracts hens. The hens run to the male and the male drops the food, allowing the hens to eat it. This behaviour is often followed by courtship behaviour and mating. Food calling is enhanced by the presence of a hen, compared with being alone.

Evans and Marler (1994) were able to show that the enhancement of calling in the presence of the hen is not just a general effect on the motivation (or arousal) of the cockerel to feed because the presence of the hen increases the food calling but not pecking at food. In other words, the presence of the hen had a specific effect on signalling about food but did not have any effect on behaviour not used for signalling. It would seem, therefore, that the cockerel signals with the intention of alerting the hen to the presence of food and does not simply emit calls automatically on the sight of food.

Added to this, Evans (1997) has now shown that the hen looks for food on the ground when she hears the food call. Evans observed the behaviour of a hen when she was played the food call through a loudspeaker. On hearing the call she put her head close to the floor and walked around as if looking for food, even though there were no grains of food present on the floor of the cage in which she was tested. Thus, her searching for food was triggered by hearing the food call specifically and not by having caught sight of any grains of food on the floor. The receiver of the signal has responded in a specific manner.

It is most important to note that either a male or female conspecific (member of the same species) is an effective audience for a cockerel to signal the presence of an aerial predator, whereas only a female is an effective audience for the food call. This demonstrates even more specificity of the particular situation in which the cockerel will produce calls and it also makes sense for the survival of the species. Both males and females can benefit by being alerted to the presence of an aerial predator but food calling is used by males to attract females as a prelude to courtship. In other words, the audience is not a simple factor of presence or absence but one with specific relevance to the particular social context and, it would seem, the intent of the signaller.

In the examples given so far, calling is enhanced by the presence of an audience but this is not the case for all types of calling. The presence of an audience has no effect on the amount of calling the cockerel gives when he sees a predator on the ground. Marler and Evans (1996) reason that this is because the ground-alarm call is not only used to alert other members of the species to the presence of a predator but also to confront the predator itself, and hopefully drive it away. This contrasts with the aerial-alarm call, which is associated with behaviour that would hide the bird from the predator. The aerial-alarm call is a thin sound that fades in and out, making its source very difficult to locate, whereas the ground-predator alarm call is conspicuous, abrupt, repeated and easy to locate. It appears to be designed to capture the ground predator's attention and is accompanied by behaviour that might just make the predator decide to look elsewhere for a meal.

Drawing attention to itself would appear to be the only strategy to adopt by a bird confronted by a predator on the ground. Chickens can fly far enough to get away and they can run fast too but the strutting and calling display directed at the predator might be a less energetically costly way of signalling to the predator that the bird could escape if approached. The situation may resemble that of the Thomson's gazelle, which engages in stotting behaviour towards predators. Stotting is leaping in the air and signals how fit the gazelle is and thus how it could escape (this will be discussed in more detail in Chapter Six).

Fleeing would be the only other alternative available to the chicken approached by a predator on the ground. This strategy might follow the strutting and alarm calling at a moment when the bird's calling and strutting activity may, perhaps, have put the predator off-guard. Whatever the reason for the bird's strutting around when confronted by a predator on the ground, there is just as much reason to strut around and make the ground-predator alarm call irrespective of whether an audience is present or not. This might explain why having an audience has no effect on ground-alarm calling.

The difference of the audience effect on aerial-alarm versus ground-alarm calling illustrates that calling is very specific to the context in which it occurs, and that there is no single, simple set of rules that the bird follows to control its vocalisations. Although this does not prove beyond all doubt that birds communicate intentionally, it certainly indicates that they may do so. Also, there is further evidence to suggest that chickens can control when and what they communicate and this finding concerns the use of calls to deceive another individual, as we will discuss below.

Deception

The use of signals to deceive another is, perhaps, the most sophisticated form of signalling. In the most developed form of deception, the deceiver may know the usual context of the signal and then use it in an unusual context with the intent of deceiving another animal. It appears that animals sometimes communicate deceptively but it is very difficult to prove beyond doubt that they have done so intentionally. Nevertheless, there is some evidence indicating that animals do engage in deception with intent, as outlined by Rogers (1997).

Gyger and Marler (1988) have observed that cockerels sometimes make food calls when no food is present. They appear to do this only when the hen is far enough away to be unable to see whether food is actually present where the cockerel is located. On hearing the call the hen approaches the cockerel, presumably to search for food in that vicinity; thus, by issuing the food call when no food is present, the cockerel can deceive the hen into approaching provided she is at a distance and cannot see that he is cheating. According to Gyger and Marler, the cockerel does not use food calls deceptively when the hen is close enough to see that he is signalling deceptively.

These are interesting observations but more experiments need to be carried out to decide exactly whether the calls are used deceptively. For example, it is possible that the cockerel emits food calls to attract the hen only when she is further away because he is more motivated to obtain her company when she is at a greater distance, rather than because he has figured out that he can deceive her only when she is further away. Nevertheless, these are new and interesting approaches that attempt to unravel the difficult problem of intentionality in animal communication and they lay a basis for more research in the area (see the 1997 paper by Christopher Evans for more discussion of this).

Other examples of deception have been reported by ethologists studying the behaviour of animals in their natural environment. It is not our intention to list them all here but we draw attention to one form of deception that has been observed in many different species—that is, issuing a warning call or behaving as if a predator were nearby when there is no evidence that that is the case. We refer to this as 'crying wolf' and remember the story of the boy who cried 'Wolf!' too often and so was ignored when he really needed help. Deception is effective only if it is used very rarely.

Rare though it may be, predator-warning behaviour appears to be used in many species to distract the attention of the receiver who is eating a favoured food and then the deceiver moves in to grab the food for itself. The Arctic fox has been observed to use warning calls in this manner, and so have domestic dogs and certain species of birds (described in detail in Rogers' *Minds of their Own* 1997). In his book *The Thinking Ape*, Richard Byrne (1995) describes many observations of deception in primates. One incident involved pretence that a predator was nearby: a baboon being chased by another baboon was observed to stop and look around as if there were a lion or other predator in the near distance and, when it did so, its pursuer stopped and looked around too, giving the pursued one time to escape. Seeing no evidence of a predator in the area, Byrne interpreted this behaviour as deception. The pursued individual had manipulated the pursuer by signalling incorrect information.

Deception is perhaps the most complex form of communication. It can occur only when a communication

45

system is firmly in place and usually functions in a consistent and reliable (referred to as 'honest') fashion. Individuals who are detected signalling dishonestly are punished or their signals ignored. Deception is a complex and risky form of communication. Its existence suggests intentionality of communication.

Mimicry is a form of deception. Wolfgang Wickler (1968) has described the way in which certain nonpoisonous butterflies mimic the appearance of poisonous ones so that they gain protection from avian predators that have learnt to avoid the poisonous butterflies. In this case, the deception is definitely unintentional because the colouration of the mimics is determined by genes. Other forms of mimicry may, however, be intentional. We do not yet know for certain but some forms of vocal mimicry in birds may be used to deceive predators and this may well be intentional. By mimicking the vocalisations of their predators some avian species may signal that the territory is occupied by another member of the predator's species and so prevent the predator from moving in. There is some evidence that this occurs but much more research is needed before we can say anything conclusive. We will discuss mimicry further in Chapters Three and Five.

Alarm calls to refer to predators

We have discussed the different calls produced by chickens and vervet monkeys to warn other members of their species of specific classes of predators. These signals are termed 'referential signals' because they appear to be analogous to human words used to refer to animals, objects or events. A number of other species, likewise, use different calls to refer to different types of predators (see Macedonia & Evans 1993).

In a refinement of this ability, prairie dogs (*Cynomys gunnisoni*) can actually signal the details of a predator in their alarm calls. Slobodchikoff and colleagues (1991), at Northern Arizona University, recorded the alarm calls that prairie dogs made as humans approached at a walking pace. As this species has been preyed on by humans for more than a hundred years, the experiment was relatively natural or, at least, relevant to the species. The human 'predators' wore different clothes in different tests, white laboratory coats or coloured shirts, and different people were involved. By recording the calls made by the prairie dogs and then analysing different detailed features of the calls, the researchers were able to show that the prairie dogs might be able to distinguish one individual human from another and that they might incorporate information about the physical features of individual predators into their alarm calls. This is an interesting result but it needs to be supported by tests showing that the prairie dogs actually use this information when they hear the different signals. If so, it tells us that animals are not only perceiving much more detail than we might have thought but also that they are signalling this information to each other. The researchers need to use playback experiments to see whether the prairie dogs actually use the detailed information encoded in the alarm signals.

Ring-tailed lemurs (*Lemur catta*) produce differentiated alarm calls to alert their group members to an aerial or a ground predator but they also have a general call, a relatively soft 'glup' sound, that they produce when they first catch sight of any predator or, indeed, when they perceive any startling visual or auditory stimulus. This seems to be a general alert signal to the group. If an aerial predator has been detected they follow the 'glup' by loud calls, first rasps and then shrieks when the predator is within attack range. If the predator is a carnivore (ground predator), the 'glup' is followed by 'clicks' and 'yaps'. Thus, the lemurs signal information about aerial versus ground predators and also about the proximity of the predator.

The ground squirrels of California (*Spermophilus beecheyi*) produce 'chatter' calls when they see a predator on the ground and 'whistles' when an eagle or hawk flies overhead, but their calls are not as specific as the alarm calls of chickens or the eagle and snake alarm calls of vervet monkeys. Sometimes they chatter when they see a hawk in the distance or whistle when they are being chased by a carnivore. These apparent errors in reference to specific predators may, in fact, be conveying more detail about the situation in general. They may indicate the urgency of the situation and thus convey information about potential versus imminent danger rather than simply saying 'Hawk' or 'Dog'. Thus, while some species have specific calls to refer to different predators, just as we use words for them, others may signal the urgency of the situation instead.

The role of emotion in signalling

We have presented evidence showing that animals do not simply vocalise in an uncontrolled manner as an expression of their emotions. Nevertheless, emotional state does affect their signalling, just as it affects speech and other forms of communication in humans. The variation in calls made by ground squirrels may, as mentioned above, indicate the urgency of the situation, depending on the proximity of the predator and perhaps also the behaviour of the predator. The emotional state of the signaller may be the factor that determines these particular variations in signalling. When the squirrel is very afraid it may whistle and when it is only mildly afraid it may chatter. In general, hawks may be of greater threat than ground predators and thus are more likely to elicit high levels of fear and whistle calls, but when a hawk is far away it elicits only a chatter. By contrast, being chased by a carnivore would be a highly fear-inducing situation and whistles are elicited in this context.

Similar systems of calling have been reported for other species: for example, the black-winged stilt (*Himantopus himantopus*), a wading bird, has two types of alarm signal depending on the distance of the predator from the bird's location. Again, increasing fear may lead to a switch from one call type to another. Similarly, as mentioned above, ring-tailed lemurs give rasping calls when an aerial predator is far away and shrieks when it is closer.

Other species vary the rate of calling with increasing risk of being caught by a predator, as found with yellow-bellied marmots (*Marmota flaviventris*). At field sites in Colorado and Utah, Daniel Blumstein and Kenneth Armitage (1997), of the University of Kansas, studied the alarm calls the marmots gave on the approach of a trained dog, a model badger, a radio-controlled badger and a walking person. The marmots made three different alarm calls but the calls did not appear to be specifically related to any of the types of predator, possibly because all the 'predators' used in the study were artificial ones. But the marmots' rate of calling increased as the predator came closer. Calling rate is, therefore, an indication of the level of fear. By playing back one of these calls at various rates, the researchers were able to show that the rate of calling did, in fact, signal the degree of risk to other marmots. Thus the receiver could interpret the meaning of the call from the calling rate.

Emotional or internal state can be influenced by hormones and this can be reflected in signalling. The amount of aerial-alarm calling by cockerels is influenced by the level of testosterone (a sex hormone) circulating in the bloodstream; this may be because the hormone changes the bird's emotional state and the way it attends to the predator.

In humans we can tell the level of emotion by the intensity and quality of the voice. This may also be the case in animals but it has not been studied to any great extent. We do, however, know that calling is more frequent and louder when animals are more aroused. The more distressed a young chick feels, the more often it peeps and the louder it peeps. A similar pattern of responses accompanies increased distress in a wide range of species, including humans. Emotional aspects of signalling may also be conveyed by other methods of communication accompanying vocalisations. Humans signal their emotional state when speaking by body posture and facial expression.

A twitch of muscles in the face or wringing of the hands can be more informative than the actual words being spoken. Animals too accompany their vocalisations with other signals that may indicate emotional state. Cockatoos, for example, raise their crests at the same time as vocalising, when they are alarmed.

In some cases, the behaviour accompanying a particular vocalisation is quite obviously another direct response to the stimulus that also elicited the vocalisation. Ground squirrels accompany their whistle calls with scurrying into their burrows. Vervet monkeys stand on their hind limbs and look down into the grass at the same time as they give the snake alarm call, look up and take to cover when making the eagle call and scamper up a tree when making the leopard call. These characteristic actions accompanying each alarm call add to the power of its meaning, and the speed or vigour with which they are performed may indicate the amount of fear that the signaller is feeling, although this has not yet been studied.

More subtle behavioural changes may accompany vocalisations. As Eckard Hess (1965) showed three decades ago, in humans, the size of the pupils in the eyes varies with emotional state and attitude. Also, humans assess the pupil size of other individuals with whom they are interacting, although they do so quite unconsciously. A greeting accompanied by dilation of the pupils is rated as positive, whereas one with constriction of the pupils is rated as negative and with distrust.

Pupil size might be an important aspect of communication in animals also. We know that it varies with the state of arousal or emotion. Some years ago Richard Gregory and Prue Hopkins (1974), of the University of Bristol, reported that the pupil size of a parrot constricted whenever she produced learnt words and also while she was listening to familiar words. There has been no research to test whether other parrots respond to the changes in pupil size but it is potentially possible that they do.

Other emotional responses such as the erection of hair

or feathers might also accompany vocalisations and signal emotional content. We have already mentioned raising of the crest in cockatoos. Most readers will be familiar with the way in which dogs raise the hair on their backs when they are angry. Unfortunately, most studies of communication in animals focus on only one aspect of signalling and ignore the complete picture, so there is little detailed information on these added aspects of signalling.

Signalling and cognition

Despite the contribution of emotions to signalling in animals, we must emphasise that signalling in animals is not purely the expression of emotions. Cognitive processes are involved in addition to emotions. By cognitive processes we mean higher levels of brain function, those that involve decision making, memory and assessment of the situation in the environment. It is possible that some signals given by some species are purely emotional, emitted without the contribution of cognition. On the other hand, it is likely that most vocalisations involve both emotional and cognitive processes, although the emotional contribution may be greater in some signals and the cognitive contribution higher in others. The balance between emotion and cognition will vary with the function of the signal and the context in which it is given. This is likely to be as true for the vocalisations of animals as it is for those of humans.

The emotional content of human speech holds our interest and adds to the meaning of the communication. This is clearly demonstrated by the contrast between computer-generated speech and human speech. Computer-generated speech is monotonous, with reduced meaning, and our attention wanders. Most animal vocalisations depend on varying contributions of emotions and cognition. The food calls given by many species (such as chimpanzees, macaque monkeys and chickens) are not monotonous and identical vocalisations produced in all cases that food is found. Instead they vary according to how much food is there and the quality of it. Chickens, for example, produce food calls at higher rates when the food is of the preferred kind, but other aspects of the call are varied in other species. The information about quantity and quality may be generated by the emotional state of the chicken producing the calls, as both more food and food of better quality may increase that bird's excitement.

At the same time as expressing the emotions, signals can be referential (which requires one form of cognition) and they can be emitted or suppressed depending on the presence or absence of an audience, or on other external factors. The relative importance of emotional versus referential processes varies with the particular call. For example, the leopard alarm call of vervet monkeys appears to have more emotional content than either the eagle alarm call or the snake alarm call—the leopard alarm call has been observed to occur occasionally in aggressive social interactions and sometimes when a raptor swoops down at the monkey, whereas the eagle and snake alarm calls have never been heard unless the specific predator to which they refer is present. Each of the latter two calls, therefore, has a unitary meaning, whereas the leopard alarm call appears to have more than one meaning.

Joseph Maccdonia and Christopher Evans (1993) have, however, reasoned that the leopard alarm call does not simply signal the monkey's level of excitement or fear, as in the case of the whistle calls of ground squirrels, because the same leopard call is produced whenever the monkeys see a leopard regardless of what degree of threat it actually poses (i.e. whether the leopard is asleep, hunting, attacking, moving away or towards). It could, of course, be argued that a leopard causes maximum levels of fear irrespective of what it is doing, and that may be why there is no variation in calling.

So far, most research on the referential use of vocalisations in animals has focused on signalling about the presence of predators or food, but much of the communication in animals must be concerned with social relationships. Although survival depends on alerting con-specifics to predators and food, social interactions are an equally important aspect of an animal's life. It follows that a considerable amount of communication must occur about social situations but virtually nothing is known about these forms of communication. Certainly, Cheney and Seyfarth (1985, 1990) have shown that vervet monkeys are aware of the social relationship between a mother and her off-spring: when an infant vocalises in distress, other monkeys turn to look at the mother of the infant rather than going to its assistance themselves. This is an example of active suppression of responding to a signal by monkeys who are not related to the infant. It shows that social signalling depends on the social context.

There are many other ways in which vervet monkeys, and other species, may communicate about social situations in an active manner but, unfortunately, we know nothing of this potentially rich field of communication. As Sue Savage-Rumbaugh of the Yerkes Institute said during a seminar that she presented at the University of New England in December 1997, apes may be less interested in communicating about objects than are humans and more interested in communicating about social matters.

We are far from understanding communication at the social level but it is reasonable to say that, although emotional states may be an aspect of social communication in animals, communication may also be generated by cognitive processes.

Animals that understand human language

It would help us to find out for certain whether animals communicate intentionally if we could ask them what they intended to communicate and they could reply using com-munication signals that we could understand. There are two potential ways of achieving this two-way communication: either we could learn to use the communication signals of the animal species we wished to study or we could teach the animal to use some form of human language. As we have not yet been successful in understanding more than rudimentary aspects of animal communication signals, the latter has presented itself as the best option. Apes have been taught to communicate with humans using American sign language, or by pointing to symbols that represent words. They have not been taught verbal communication using spoken English, for example, because the vocal apparatus of apes is very different from that of humans and does not allow them to make the same range of vocalisations that we do. This does not mean that apes' vocal abilities are limited—they can and do use a range of complex calls, with a vocal range extending to very high frequencies. Birds can produce the same range of sounds as humans and they can be taught to communicate with humans using vocal signals, as was a parrot, called Alex.

We will discuss intentional communication in apes first. Allen and Beatrix Gardner, of the University of Nevada, trained several chimpanzees to communicate with humans using American sign language, beginning in 1966 with one called Washoe (see Gardner et al. 1989). The chimpanzees learnt to use signs to refer to objects and individuals and all of them acquired vocabularies that allowed them to express requests, such as 'Icecream, hurry gimme' (to use the Gardners' translation), 'You tickle me Washoe', 'Please flower', 'Please blanket out' (requesting a change in location of a blanket then in the cupboard), 'You me out' (a request for the carer and chimpanzee to go outside) and 'Open help' (requesting assistance in opening a lock or a bottle). By the chimpanzees' frustrated behaviour when these requests were not performed, compared with when they were, it was clear that these were intentional forms of communication. The chimpanzees also announced when the next activity in the daily routine should occur with statements such as 'Time vacuum', 'Time toothbrush' and 'Time Dar out' (Dar being the name of one of the chimpanzees). This announcement of a pending event is an aspect of awareness of the future also indicating intentionality. Emotion entered into the signing—more emotive events evoked more signing—but cognition was obviously a major aspect of their communication.

To convince critics that the chimpanzees were expressing genuine requests and were coming up with answers to questions by use of their own powers of cognition, it was necessary for the Gardners to prove that the chimpanzees were not using subtle cues given inadvertently by their human carers. By responding to cues produced by the humans in their presence, the apes might appear to be communicating intelligently and intentionally but would merely be performing some sort of clever mimicry. In other words, they might be similar to Clever Hans, the horse that was once thought to be able to read numbers written on a board and to count them out by tapping his foot on the floor. Later it was found that the horse used subtle cues that his owner supplied unknowingly (e.g. the blink of an eyelid when the horse tapped the required number of times). Clever Hans could not perform the task when his owner was not present.

To test whether a similar use of cues might be occurring with the chimpanzees, the Gardners designed an experiment in which the chimpanzees had to name objects shown to them on a video monitor. Their responses were recorded by a human who could not see the screen and did not know what the chimpanzees were observing. There was no human who knew what was on the television screen present in the room with the chimpanzee. In this controlled experiment, the chimpanzees were able to name objects accurately. Therefore, their use of sign language was self-generated and not some form of mimicry or associative learning.

The chimpanzees also used the sign language they had learnt to tell humans things they did not already know. For example, when very young, Washoe dropped one of her toys into a hole in the inside wall of the caravan in which she lived. That night, when Allen Gardner visited her, she attracted his attention to a part of the wall below the hole and signed 'Open, open' many times over. From this communication Allen deduced what had happened and retrieved the toy. Washoe had used sign language to communicate something really new to a human. This shows genuine communication with intention. Again, there is no question of the chimpanzee communicating merely by reading subtle cues given by her carer. Although this was claimed rather vehemently by several researchers in the field at one time, a complete analysis of the data accumulated by the Gardners shows that this narrow interpretation is most unlikely to be correct. Moreover, more recent findings by other researchers who have trained apes to use language support the conclusion that apes can learn to communicate with humans intentionally, creatively and intelligently.

Sue Savage-Rumbaugh has trained chimpanzees and a bonobo (a rare species of chimpanzee, *Pan paniscus*, also known as a pygmy chimpanzee) to communicate with humans by pointing to symbols on a board (lexigram symbols) (see Savage-Rumbaugh & Lewin 1994). She has said that, while the sign-language-trained chimpanzees used their acquired language mainly to manipulate humans, the symbol-trained chimpanzees seemed to have more of a two-way communication with humans. While this claim would need to be proven, if it is correct it might stem from the fact that the signing chimpanzees were trained by giving them small food rewards when they signed correctly, and thus they would associate signing with getting a food reward from humans. The other factor that might be important is that humans communicated with the symbol-trained apes using spoken language, not sign language as is generally the case in the chimpanzees trained to use sign language. The combined use of speech by humans and symbols by the apes might have facilitated the human–animal exchange because humans could speak to the apes directly using their natural form of communication. Whatever the reason, the symbol-trained apes have impressive two-way communication with humans and they are able to use that communication to refer to events that have occurred in the past or to talk about other individuals not present at the time. This is clear referential use of communication.

Not only is meaning important to these apes (i.e. referential use of symbols) but also syntax (grammatical word order in sentences). This was discovered by Savage-Rumbaugh in her work with the bonobo, Kanzi (Savage-Rumbaugh & Lewin 1994). Kanzi learnt to communicate, by pointing to symbols, by being present at an early age when his mother was being taught to use them. He learnt to use the symbols to generate language in much the same way that a human child acquires language. He also acquired the ability to understand spoken English. In a sense he is now trilingual because he is able to understand spoken English, use symbolic language and, most likely, use his own 'chimpanzee' mode of communication. This is more than we expect of the average human child.

He also learnt to understand the syntax of English as Savage-Rumbaugh was able to show by the following experiment. Kanzi was given instructions via headphones by a person in another room who could not see him. In the same room as Kanzi was another person who did not know what instruction Kanzi had received and who recorded his behaviour. Kanzi was instructed to perform a task using pidgin English (e.g. 'Go get orange testing room') or syntactically correct English (e.g. 'Go and get the orange from the testing room') and the rapidity of his responses was recorded. The results demonstrated that he responded more rapidly and more effectively when the syntactically correct instruction was given than when pidgin English was used. Therefore he has acquired understanding of not only the meaning of words (semantics) but also the structure (syntax) of English language. The symbolic language by which he has learnt to communicate with humans does not permit this expression of syntax but he does process and respond to syntax. In fact, Kanzi can understand numerous sentences in spoken English.

This remarkable demonstration of Kanzi's ability to understand human language is sufficient for us to say that apes possess the ability to process language and they might use this ability in their own vocalisations or other forms of communication. It even raises the possibility that other species that live in close contact with humans understand what humans are saying even though they cannot themselves speak. In his work with dolphins at the University of Hawaii, Louis Herman and his colleagues recognised this possibility of comprehension in the absence of audible or visible production of signals, although in this case he was considering the dolphins' ability to understand the gestural 'language' of humans rather than speech (Herman et al. 1993). Dolphins can follow complex commands presented to them as gestures asking them to perform various acts in sequence, even though they have not been trained to produce vocal or other communication that can be understood by humans. In saying this, we must not overlook the dolphins' own complex vocal and other forms of communication, which might also share aspects of human language (see Chapter Four for more details).

It is possible that many species that live in close contact with humans acquire some comprehension of both the semantics and syntax of human language, even though they cannot produce it. We all know that dogs, for example, understand simple commands but we might now speculate that they understand much more of the conversations we have in their presence, and the same may be true of pet birds. In fact, a study by Millicent Ficken, Elizabeth Hailman and Jack Hailman, of the University of Wisconsin, has shown that chickadees (*Parus sclateri*, an avian species in Mexico) sequence their different calls in particular ways, according to rules and the context in which the calls are given. This is a simple form of syntax, as the researchers state (Ficken et al. 1994). It is probable that many other examples of syntax will be found in the communication systems of animals, and it need not be only in vocal communication.

Of all the species that could have been chosen for the research on teaching human language to animals, it is not surprising that apes were selected. Apes are closest to humans genetically and in terms of evolution; so it was considered they would be more likely to be able to learn to communicate using language than any other species. Irene Pepperberg, however, saw potential in training a species far removed from humans—the African grey parrot (*Psittacus erithacus*). Parrots have an advantage over apes in that they can mimic human speech vocally and might be able to communicate directly without the need for an interface of signs or symbols.

In her laboratory at the University of Arizona, Pepperberg (1990a, 1990b) began by training a parrot called Alex. The training had to differ from the usual way in which parrots are taught to mimic speech. Instead of mindlessly repeating words or phrases over and over to the bird quite out of context and therefore without particular meaning to the bird, she engaged in simple but meaningful interactions in front of Alex. For example, one person would ask 'Where is the key?' and another would hold it up with a reply such as 'Here is the key'. The first person would then ask 'What colour is the key?' and the other person would state the colour, and so on with objects of different shapes and textures. When Alex began to use words, he was given the objects that he asked for. He was also rewarded by the human telling him he was a good bird.

With this training, Alex has learnt to name up to 100 objects and to answer questions correctly about their shape, colour and texture. He can also count and, when presented with an array of objects of various shapes and colours on a tray, he can say how many of the objects are, for example, green triangles or blue four-corners (by which he means cubes). Alex also expresses desires, such as 'I want peanut' or 'Come here' (more detail on Alex is given in Chapter Three). In all aspects of his communication, he performs as well as the language-trained apes, which supports our suggestion that many species may be capable of understanding aspects of human language. This comment aside, the relevant point about the research with Alex is that he uses his acquired vocabulary to communicate intelligently with humans. He is not simply emitting signals mindlessly, out of context or unintentionally.

Conclusion

In 1975, the primatologist Premack asserted that, whereas humans have both affective and symbolic communication, all other species, except those tutored by humans, have only affective communication (Premack 1975). By 'affective' communication he meant communication about emotions in an uncontrolled way. At the time he wrote, apes had already been taught to communicate using sign language (Premack himself had been part of the research program) and their abilities to communicate symbolically were known. Instead of extrapolating this knowledge to communication by species using their own species-specific patterns of communication, Premack saw the language-trained apes as exceptions that had acquired something extra as a result of their contact with humans. The more recent research of Marler, Evans and colleagues on vocalisations in chickens discounts Premack's claim. They have shown that alarm and food calls are not simply produced automatically without control (Marler & Evans 1996). We might, therefore, conclude that the apes who have been taught to communicate using signed or symbolic forms that humans can understand tell us something important about their species and, in that respect at least, are not special or exceptions to their species.

The research on Kanzi and his ability to comprehend the syntax of spoken English has led us to suggest that many other species might have similar abilities despite the fact that they cannot speak to us or communicate by signing or using symbols. We would go a step further and suggest that the ability to understand the syntax of spoken English indicates that bonobos, at least, must communicate using their own species-specific signals (vocal and gestural) in ways similar to human language. We base this prediction on the fact that a species that can comprehend human language is also likely to have similar processing capabilities that are used for its own forms of communication; in turn, this means that the species must produce language-like communication. The fact that language-like production of communication has not yet been found in animals tells us only that far too little research on natural communication has, so far, taken place—it certainly does not tell us that it does not exist.

In fact, detailed examination of the vocalisations of different species frequently reveals that humans are unable to distinguish between calls that actually differ from each other. In other words, we may not hear differences that the animals hear. Many years ago, this was found to be the case for the most common call of Japanese macaque monkeys (*Macaca fuscata*), known as the 'coo' call. The monkeys make 'coos' in a variety of social situations and, although these all sound the same to human listeners, detailed analysis revealed that the calls differed in each situation. More recently the same has been found for the trill calls of spider monkeys (*Ateles geoffroyi*): although all trills sound the same to us, spider monkeys can tell exactly which individual made the call. These examples should indicate to us that there is much more in the vocal communication of animals than we hear or understand.

CHAPTER THREE

COMMUNICATION IN BIRDS

Birds have inspired human imagination. To fly like a bird is a dream as old as the flight of Icarus in Greek mythology. The white dove has come to symbolise peace; birds also symbolise freedom. Bird feathers have been used to signal special powers or to confer a special status on the human wearer. Birds feature in many human dances—many cultures have prided themselves on being able to mimic birdsong and bird displays. Human fascination may also arise from having something in common with birds. Humans and birds share a strong investment in communication by vocalisation. In fact, the complexity of song and communication systems developed by birds and by humans has no equal among vertebrates, except for whales and dolphins.

Birdsong had been studied and described long before scientists took a scholarly interest in it. Today, the study of birdsong is a substantial field in its own right. It is studied for the sake of learning about its communicative value, but also because it is aesthetically pleasing. It may be described in terms of its structure as well as its function. We may be interested in the acquisition of song or in how and where song is produced. Ethologists are interested in birdsong in relation to questions of territory, reproductive strategies and sexual reproduction.

In evolutionary terms different species of birds may be as far apart from each other as ungulates are from humans.

The first bird evolved in the Jurassic period. Although most birds evolved later, in the Cretaceous period, millions of years separate the appearance of the various species. For instance, the first known occurrence of some flightless birds, including species of game birds and waterfowl, may have been about 110 million years ago, separated from parrots by about ten million years. While most birds of prey developed about 70 million years ago, they evolved about 30 million years later than songbirds. Among the 'newcomers', appearing in the tertiary period a mere 50 million years ago, were albatrosses, frigatebirds, penguins and petrels. Thus, when humans began to evolve about four million years ago, the air, the ground and the waters were already occupied by winged and beaked species.

In popular imagination it is often thought that everything that has wings and lays eggs is one of the same kind, but their evolutionary distance and differences in behaviour make this as unlikely as trying to determine similarities between mice and tigers. Not just for reasons of appearance have birds been seen as a unitary set of species: the history of ideas has also played a role. Descartes' notion that only humans are 'complete' beings by virtue of their ability to think had particularly bad repercussions for birds. A false impression was created that birds are essentially like mechanistic toys. Birds have been used as colourful decorations in living rooms or as self-propelled music-boxes on mantelpieces, just to adorn human dwellings, with little thought of the live bird.

Outside captivity, birds also gave impetus for negative imagery, such as symbolically conveying evil (e.g. the crow on the witch's back). Vultures are a symbol of death and any haunted house worth its reputation has birds flying from it, dark and menacing and distinguished by sharp beaks and claws. The links with bats and prehistoric monsters are established here. This negative imagery of birds contrasts with the positive association with their flight and vocalisations.

Unfortunately, whether or not the imagery associated with birds is positive, this has had little influence on overturning the view of birds as 'mechanistic' toys. This has a number of consequences for studies of communication in birds. It influences what we prejudge as being the capability of birds and affects what we discern as human observers. In certain avian species, basic vocal signals may be innate and automatic. However, in more evolved avian species, such as the Psittacine group (parrots, cockatoos, budgerigars), Corvids (ravens) and the Cracticidae (Australian magpies, currawongs, butcherbirds), studies have shown that many of the vocalisation skills are learnt behaviours, the mastery of which is part of the success in finding a partner, breeding, and succeeding in holding territory. As we saw in Chapter Two, there is nothing automatic about the production of vocalisations even in the chicken (*Gallus gallus domesticus*), even though their vocalisations are simple compared with songbirds and many other species. Hence, we may often be dealing with learnt, complex vocalisations and very complex social interactions (we discuss this in detail in Chapter Five).

We are only just beginning to understand the complexity of bird communication. Researchers who have shown that a variety of birds are capable of complex communication have fought traditional views. The work by Irene Pepperberg (1990a, 1990b) and her African grey parrot Alex is one example. Alex communicates with the researcher using English words. He can count and discriminate shapes, colours and objects. He can understand commands and express wishes (see Chapter Two). These capabilities appear to be the result of thinking (or consciousness) rather than automatic responses. Alex, the parrot, may well be on a par with the great apes in his abilities to communicate and reason.

Many other avian species may have abilities similar to those of Alex. Our galah, for instance, after we have been away at night, always asks on our return 'Where have you been?' He never asks this question at any other time. It could be suggested that he has learnt to produce this vocalisation only in a particular context, the return of a familiar human, but we might also describe the spoken words of humans in this way, although we know this is not the explanation. The extensive research by Irene Pepperberg on Alex indicates that he has learnt to use English words to communicate in a comprehensive way, not simply by mindless association of certain words with certain events.

One famous Australian corella, a particularly argumentative species, has learnt to argue with and even shout at its owner in human language. The studies by Konrad Lorenz (1966) on corvids (European ravens) and Kaplan's recent studies on the Australian magpie show similar complexity of communication (more of this later).

Choosing a mode for communicating

When we speak of communication in birds, it is customary to order the means of communication (visual, auditory, olfactory) according to a hierarchy from most to least important for the species. In some classic studies it was found that, in relation to other means of communication, acoustic signals are of prime importance in most species of birds. This was shown to be the case in the domestic hen's recognition of her chick. When a transparent bell was placed over a small chicken, preventing the hen from hearing its calls, the hen paid no attention to the distressed chick. A turkey, also deprived of auditory cues, failed to recognise her own offspring, and consequently attacked and even killed them, as she would any intruder. Hence, in some contexts and in some avian species, acoustic signalling is superior to visual signalling.

Recognition need not involve sophisticated vocalisation patterns but may require excellent hearing. The excellent hearing of many birds may also be used to find food. For instance, the Australian magpie (*Gymnorhina tibicen*) locates its food largely by sound. Its hearing is so good that it can locate scarab larvae moving in the soil several inches under the surface. The Australian tawny frogmouth

(*Podargus strigoides*) could theoretically find its food blind-fold. It can hear the rustle of beetles and cockroaches in the undergrowth from the height of a tree branch. We might expect acoustic signals to bear characteristics relevant to the bird's social and ecological environment, and also to its hearing capacity, but this is not necessarily so. Australian magpies have very intense, high-amplitude calls and song, which seems extravagant given their exceptional hearing. By contrast, the tawny frogmouth uses low-amplitude and low-frequency sounds to communicate. Tawny frogmouths, unlike magpies, are nocturnal. In the stillness of an Australian bush night, the repetitious hoot of the tawny frogmouth can be heard for miles.

Visual signals

In addition to vocalisations, both magpies and tawny frogmouths use visual signals to communicate. One of the authors (Kaplan) raises and rehabilitates injured and abandoned birds. Kaplan found that neither magpies nor tawny frogmouths recognised her by auditory cues alone. If her clothes had changed, even though her auditory cues remained the same, birds of both species showed fear responses as if she were an entirely different person. Of course, a change of clothing may be a difficult concept for a bird to accommodate, because birds rarely change plumage colour and patterns (other than from nestling to adult or, in some species, from season to season, e.g. the partridge in Europe and the male superb fairy wren in Australia). When Kaplan took her regular animal-feeding clothes into the aviary and changed from her 'new' to her regular feeding clothes in front of the magpie, the bird watched with great intensity every move that was made during the transformation. Thereafter, the magpie never again showed any fear response when different clothes were worn. Instead, it watched her face and listened carefully to the voice and then showed the same behaviours of familiarity as with the old clothes. A tawny frogmouth was given the same clothes-changing performance but never abandoned its fear response when new clothes were worn.

A recent study by Patrice Adret, of the University of St Andrews, has shown that visual stimuli (in the form of video images) have reinforcing properties in zebra finches (*Taeniopygia guttata*), although the study allowed auditory cues as well (Adret 1997). Merely showing the head of another male zebra finch on screen roused the experimental bird to song. Bengalese finches (*Lonchura striata domestica*), investigated by Shigeru Watanabe of Keio University in Tokyo, were found to rely predominantly on visual cues for discriminative behaviour. The auditory signals in his experiments provided purposely ambiguous information and in those cases the bird's attention switched to visual signals which were not ambiguous (Watanabe 1993).

Although birds use vocalisations extensively for communicative purposes, they are by no means their only way of communicating. Visual communication is used widely by birds, requiring suitable eyesight to perceive the visual signals. There is a tremendous diversity in optical designs and retinal structures across avian species. Some species even have infrared and/or ultraviolet vision. Owls and a variety of other nocturnal species (such as tawny frogmouths and owlet nightjars) can see at very low intensity of light. Diurnal birds of prey have probably the best long-distance sight of any species.

Most bird species have limited movement of the eyeball but this is compensated for by flexibility of head movements. The eye of the barn owl, for instance, is fixed rather firmly in its socket but the head can move by 270 degrees, vertically and horizontally. There are only two bird species so far investigated that show extensive movement of the eyeball. One is the bittern which, in 'freezing' position (head and beak up, neck stretched), can turn the eyes forward and downwards to see below its beak and straight ahead in binocular vision. Another is the snipe which can turn its eyes upward to watch a bird overhead without moving its head at all.

The eyes of birds are often at the side of the head and therefore a good deal of visual information is obtained in monocular vision. This provides a large visual field, including above and, in some species, behind the head of the bird. This kind of vision is of great advantage for survival, but it is not clear whether it serves any communicative function. Certainly, birds make use of lateral (or broadside) displays that would use the lateral field of vision.

Like mammals, avian species have a wide range of body postures available for signalling a message by visual means. Head bobbing, arching of the neck, extending the wings outwards, and certain sorts of running, stomping and crouching postures may be used in both agonistic and courtship behaviours; that is, the same posture can have embedded in it the potential for flight and attraction. Many courtship rituals rely on rapid changes in body posture. We give examples of these in Chapter Six.

As we saw in Chapter One, one of the best known and most dramatic courtship rituals largely relying on motion and body posture is performed by the grebes (*Podiceps* ssp.) as a dance on water. The sequence is rather complex: In horned grebes (*Podiceps auritus*) the male 'bounces' forward, dives several times, then both male and female rise to full height by treading water, facing each other in what is sometimes referred to as a 'penguin' display; they continue to dance in that posture until finally swimming apart. The village weaver male (*Ploceus cucullatus*) uses a wing- and head-pointing display to attract a female's attention not only to himself but to the nest he has built. There are many bird species that use dance or ritualised movement as part of their courtship display. Lyrebirds (*Menuridae* sp.) are famous for their dancing as well as vocal displays (see Robinson & Curtis 1996).

Signalling with plumage

Feathers are often used for signalling. Although plumage colour is not a universal factor in recognition of the sex of a bird, it plays this role in a large number of species. Males of many species use it to attract a mate. Recognition of sex, in some species, may occur exclusively by visual cues—plumage colour or eye colour. For instance, the red breast of the male European robin functions as a unitary signal. Even models placed on a branch provoked attack when the breast was red, but not if the red was missing. As Glenn-Peter Saetre and Tore Slagsvold from Oslo found in experiments with caged pied flycatchers (*Ficedula hypoleuca*), when they painted a pied flycatcher female in the colours of the male, all other males treated the bird as if it were male. A male painted as a female was treated by the others as a female. This identification was maintained even when the song of the male was played in conjunction with the male bird painted as a female (Saetre & Slagsvold 1992). It is worth noting here that some male pied flycatchers naturally have plumage colouration that is closer to that of the female. In free-ranging birds, males will treat such birds as if they were female and may even engage in courtship rituals for their benefit. Males equipped with a plumage colour that mimics that of a female can accrue territorial advantages. They may invade a territory without encountering the aggression of a competing male and may succeed in staying.

Apart from sexual recognition, plumage colour and patterns may signal such things as individual identification, dominance status and mating readiness. While sexual recognition and individual identification as a result of plumage are passive, pregiven signals which are genetically determined, dominance status and mating readiness require some additional, active social communication to get their meanings across. Birds of paradise, for instance, go to extraordinary lengths to display their plumage. As mentioned in Chapter One, the male Victoria's riflebird (*Ptiloris victoriae*) will choose a sunny, exposed part of the rainforest and rhythmically display tail or wing feathers, performing a fascinating dance, with colours flashing in the sun, that will attract a female to come close for inspection. He will then proceed with his display but, this time, he half folds his wings around her (without touching her) in quick succession of left and right wing in such a way that the female becomes quite engulfed in this courtship ritual.

Perhaps the most spectacular use of feathers in signalling is shown by the peacock with tail feathers fanned out like a wheel, shimmering with each new turn of the body. As well as its iridescent green and blue colours, the peacock's tail has hundreds of eye-spots, patterns that mimic eyes, all appearing to be looking towards the centre at the body of the peacock. In Chapter One, we saw how eye-like patterns (ocelli) are used by some moths to redirect attention by birds away from the body and thereby deflect attack. The peacock uses the eye-like patterns for intra-species communication to attract a female during courtship.

An eye-like pattern is used likewise by males in one of the 43 species of the birds of paradise, the bluebird. The pattern is hidden at the abdomen and surrounded by magnificent long bright blue feathers. Only during courtship do these blue feathers with their eye-like markings (black and shiny bright red) come into full display. For this to happen, the bird needs to hang upside down on a branch and fan out all the blue feathers to expose the eye-like pattern. These then hang over the chest. He oscillates them while emitting rasping, rhythmic and mesmerising percussion sounds in quick succession.

A most unusual and complex form of visual display occurs in bowerbird species (*Chlamydera* spp.). Here the display of feathers has been replaced by decorations external to the bird. We could almost speak of tool use. Instead of, or in addition to, parading bright or striking plumage to a prospective female, males build a bower. The bower may be decorated with all manner of objects of similar colours, depending on the species' preferences. During courtship display, the male displays plumage and may vocalise and even dance, but there is the additional element of a stage, uniquely constructed specifically for the purpose of attracting a female. Like the lyrebirds, bowerbirds clear an area on the forest floor for dancing. In addition, most bowerbird species build a structure that is of no use for raising young but is used as part of their courtship display. Bowerbird males may mate with many females. Mating success is linked to the bower and the entire display, including vocalisations, dancing and construction of the site.

Signals issued by feather posture alone have rarely been studied systematically yet they may be quite important within visual range. Many birds fluff their feathers in a certain way when they are ill but they may also raise their feathers as a warning signal. Tawny frogmouths can raise all their body feathers simultaneously to make themselves look menacingly larger than they are. This display is not necessarily accompanied by a vocalisation, but it always precedes an attack and appears to be used in territorial disputes among conspecifics. In interspecies interactions, tawny frogmouths seem to 'shrink' their body size by lowering their feathers as tightly as possible to the body and by stretching their necks. The bird then gives the appearance of a branch, a camouflage that works well against a gum tree (Figure 3.1).

Facial expression

It is equally possible to attribute communicative importance to the facial expressions of birds. The idea that birds have 'facial expressions' is quite foreign to many people and there has been no systematic work done on this aspect of avian communication. The concept of a bird having a 'face' may seem strange but largely for linguistic reasons. Humans have linguistically claimed the 'face' as something uniquely human, a feature that bestows individuality. (There are now a few select mammalian species to whom we grant individuality and thus a face.) Although it is recognised that many avian species express individuality in their vocalisations, it is usually not accepted that birds do so in their appearance. But individual birds 'look' different and they do so in different contexts. Facial expression is

71

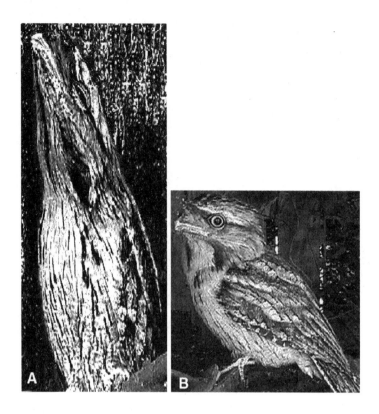

Figure 3.1 Camouflage posture of tawny frogmouth. A. Feathers sleeked down and neck and body extended in a camouflage posture. B. Neutral posture adopted by the same bird. (Photographs by G. Kaplan)

achieved either by movements of the beak or by independent positioning of feathers on the chin or above the beak, on the ear coverts, on top of the head (the crown), at the nape of the neck and, in some species, also by moving the feathers above the eyes independently of the other feathers.

Like primates (see Chapter Four), birds have open-mouth displays or, rather, open-beak displays which, together with other body signals, can be used in fear or threat displays. Tawny frogmouths use a variety of open-beak displays; the inside lining of the large oral cavity is a striking light-green colour effectively displaying the enormous size of the beak and making it look more ominous than it actually is. As a threat, a number of bird species open their beaks, even without vocalisation but sometimes associated with hissing or breathing sounds. The barn owl (*Tyto alba*), for instance, a bird that is rarely heard, emits an exhaling sound in warning while the beak is half-open and then sharply claps the beak several times, often without the slightest change in body posture or feather composition.

In galahs and crested cockatoos, movement of head feathers is very easy to detect, even from some distance. The crest goes up not just in alarm but in states of friendly arousal. The feathers that flank the beak (ear coverts) can be ruffled to express anger and possible attack. Lowering or flattening of feathers is usually associated with fear but this commonly involves the whole body rather than just the head. 'Cuddly' and babyish behaviour is often shown by fluffing feathers above and below the beak (readily observable in Australian magpies). For close, conspecific interactions, these facial expressions are powerful signals emitted with a minimum of energy expenditure.

Smell and touch

Compared with auditory and visual communication, relatively little is known of the communicative importance of the senses of smell and touch in birds. We know that many bird species preen each other, usually as an exercise in bonding and reassurance. For some avian species, particularly parrots, preening and tactile responses are very important in social interactions. In some bird species, such as the red wattlebird and the Australian magpie, nestlings immediately posthatching and prior to opening their eyes will not defecate until they feel the vibration at the nest indicating the presence of a parent. They then lift up their cloacal region towards the edge of the nest and the parent takes the firm faeces into the beak and carries it out of the nest. While this is not exactly a form of tactile communication, the tactile signal of the parent elicits the response. Later in the development of magpies, the parent may actually prompt defecation by tapping its beak directly at the offspring's cloacal region (observed by Kaplan).

Olfaction in birds is less well developed than the other senses but it is not absent. Olfactory cues have been shown to play a role in food selection in a number of species but the studies in this field are limited and it is not known whether odours are used to communicate between individuals. The sense of olfaction is unusually well developed in the New Zealand kiwi, which locates its food by sensing odours, so it is probable that olfaction is also used for communication in this species.

The tawny frogmouth can use defecation as a deterrent. The bird will fly close to the object to be deterred and will deliberately spray large quantities of extremely pungent material over or near another species. Tawnies are the skunks of the air and their warning scent, if dropped on fur or skin, is difficult to eliminate. Usually, this warning signal is reserved purely for other species and it is not clear whether tawny frogmouths themselves can actually smell their own droppings or perceive the intensity of smell of these excrements.

Even if auditory and visual cues are likely to be the most important signals in avian communication, it can at least be said that no one single sense functions entirely in isolation. Courtship displays in birds are a good example. Auditory messages are usually accompanied by visual displays which can be very elaborate, involving motion and even 'dance'. Some tactile contact may also be part of the ritual (neck touching, beak fencing or, more indirectly, by exchange of gifts).

How vocalisations are produced

Vocalisation depends on appropriate centres in the central nervous system. In addition, we distinguish a number of specific, so-called 'sound emission sites' in birds, some of which are conspicuously different from those of other vertebrates (mammals, including humans, reptiles and fish). The chief sound-producing vocal organ of a bird is called a syrinx. Although avian species also have a larynx, like humans, Suthers (1990) and others have thought that the larynx plays no significant role in sound production. However, it is still under debate to what extent supersyringeal structures, such as the trachea, larynx, tongue and even the upper and lower mandibles, may play a role in modifying sounds. The tongue may play a particular role in psittacine (parrot) species. Recent work by D.K. Patterson and Irene Pepperberg (1996) at the University of Arizona on American English vowel production in the African grey parrot has shown that this parrot can produce vowels of striking similarity to human vowels despite the very different anatomy of the psittacine vocal apparatus (e.g. no teeth or lips). Indeed, so do many parrots, as a sonogram of our galah 'speech' shows (Figure 3.2).

There are several important differences between the avian and the human vocal apparatus. The most obvious one is the location of the main sound-producing organ. The human larynx is situated in the neck, and hence is close to the mouth. The bird's syrinx, by contrast, is located well within the body of the bird. It sits at that part of the trachea (windpipe) where the bronchial branches split and go to the lung on each side of the body. Thus, a bird has two airstreams impinging on its vocal organ rather than one as in humans. The onset and termination of vocalisation (called phonation) is usually controlled by the syringeal muscles that open or close the lumen on each side of the syrinx.

The syrinx is an organ that varies in complexity from species to species. Although the precise mechanisms of sound production are not fully known, it is thought that

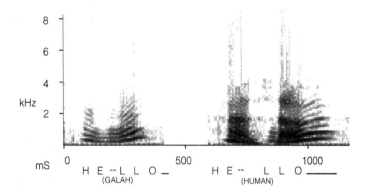

Figure 3.2   Mimicry of human speech by a galah. Although the 'hello' produced by the galah (*Cacatua roseicapilla*) is of a shorter duration than that spoken by the human, the pattern of the vocalisations are almost identical. The fundamental notes and the overtones are very similar. (Sound spectrograms by G. Kaplan)

voiced or whistled song originates from vibration of the medial tympaniform membrane. The syrinx has internal medial tympaniform membranes which are housed within the interclavicular sac, an air sac in the pleural cavity. In that location the membranes are sensitive to the air passing through from the lungs and they are controlled by the syringeal muscles and by air pressure surrounding the membranes. The elasticity and complexity of the membranes may determine the quality of sounds.

Songbirds have a very complex syringeal system, in which the syringeal muscles and the internal membranes interact to produce near pure tones (single frequency, similar to human whistles) and also, as in the lyrebird, parallel notes, seemingly played on two instruments at once. The latter produce sound from both sides of the syrinx at once, as discussed below.

In the Australian kookaburra, with its loud and raucous call, the syringeal muscles are barely developed. By contrast, the syringeal muscles of the Australian magpie are very noticeable. It is possible to trace the development of song in an Australian magpie in relation to the development of the syringeal muscles. Full song is produced only when the syringeal muscles are fully grown.

It is possible for a songbird to produce sounds from different sources at the same time—that is to use both sides of the syrinx simultaneously or independently. Roderick A. Suthers, together with a team of researchers from the universities of Indiana and Seattle, confirmed this in 1990 for the brown thrashers (*Toxostoma rufum*) and grey catbirds (*Dumetella carolinensis*). They found that in both species the frequency range of sound contributed by the right syrinx was higher than that of the left syrinx, and that phonation was frequently switched from one side to the other, not just in between syllables but within a single syllable. Simultaneous use of both sides, at least in the species they examined, resulted in syllables that are 'two-voiced'—that is, they are not harmonically related and are of different amplitude modulation. This means that one side of the syrinx is not dominant, as in the canary. In addition, some birds utilise air reservoirs in the chest as resonance chambers for the production of sound. These may be used in conjunction with the syrinx, or even in the absence of a syrinx as for instance in bustards, emus and cranes which have clavicular and cervical air sacs. The sounds produced from these air sacs appear hollow and of low frequency, like a drum being struck under water.

The sound repertoire is not exhausted at this point. Beak clapping may be developed in some species as an audible signal with communicative function. Beak clapping in storks, some owls, in the various frogmouths and in the Australian magpies is used as a strong and aggressive warning signal. Interestingly, this signal is intended for interspecies use (more on this later). Further auditory signals may be generated by the beak pecking an object (e.g. a tree) to indicate territoriality or, as in the woodpecker, for sexual communication. The male musk duck in eastern Australia (*Biziura lobata*) produces as part of his courtship ritual an odd 'plonking' sound of his feet in the water. Wingflapping and wing beating, as in wood pigeons and crested pigeons, may function as warning signals. The wing beating of a crested pigeon (*Geophaps lophotes*) is a high trill that can be heard some distance away. Not every flight motion produces this shrill sound, leading us to suspect that wing beating in crested pigeons is used for communicative purposes. Thorpe and Griffin (1962) found that flight sounds of some small birds contain ultrasound. They are therefore not audible to the human ear and probably also not to birds such as owls which prey on them, but they are certainly audible to bats and other vertebrates with ultrasonic abilities. A large number of songbird species, nearly all tits (*Parus* sp.) for example, show a behaviour called 'wing quiver' which is said to have communicative function. The wing quiver is achieved as a vibratory movement of the wings, mainly the wingtips, at a sound frequency of about 15 Hz. In the black-capped chickadees (*Parus atricapillus*) the wing quivering usually occurs in front of the nest hole before entering the nest, and Marcel Lambrechts and colleagues from the University of Wisconsin concluded from their observations that wing quivering functions as a request or invitation to the mate (Lambrechts et al. 1993).

A most unusual way to produce sound, for a bird, is tool use. The male palm cockatoo (*Probosciger aterrimus*), found only at the very tip of Australia's tropical north and in New Guinea, fashions a stick to a manageable length. He then holds it in one foot and, by drumming the stick on the tree, accompanies his very high-pitched but not very loud shrieks, dancing at the same time and swaying his head. With this triple activity—body posture swaying, vocalisation and drumming—the palm cockatoo advertises his territory.

The message in vocalisation

Many researchers still distinguish beween call and song. The assumption behind this distinction has been that calls are short and simple and are produced by both sexes throughout the year while song has at times been thought of a special category of vocalisations reserved for descriptions of male vocalisations during the breeding season. This distinction is no longer considered very useful, partly because of overlap (i.e. when does a call finish and a song begin?) and partly because not all song is related only to the breeding season. In many songbirds, but by no means all, only the males sing and they are said to do so to attract a female. Other species, however, do not confine singing to the breeding season. In the tropics, many females sing. Also, in moderate climate zones, there are some species, such as the Australian magpie, in which males and females alike sing all year round. Some birds also have a song type that could easily be regarded as consisting of a few specialised calls.

From an evolutionary perspective it has been argued that patterns of vocalisation may have become more common and more complex over time; that is, the most recently evolved species have the most complex vocalisations. The most recently evolved birds are the passerines, or songbirds, with about 56 families worldwide (from finches to scrub birds, swallows to pittas, starlings to flycatchers, pardalotes to crows, wrens to lyrebirds, warblers to currawongs—a very diverse group). Within this order we distinguish sub-oscines and oscines. Sub-oscines are birds supposedly equipped with a more primitive syringeal anatomy than 'true' songbirds. However, their song may well have become more complex over evolutionary time. To the human observer complex song may be aesthetically more pleasing, and from this it would be easy to surmise that syntax or meaning are implied in the concept of complexity. But neither complexity nor beauty of the song is in itself an indicator of content. The actual communicative value of a long, beautiful and complex song (such as that of the nightingale or of the lyrebird) may not be greater than shorter or less melodious vocalisations.

Frequencies of bird vocalisations commonly range between 2–10 kHz, within comfortable human audition range and are therefore easy to record and measure. Only a few avian species are known to produce infrasounds, such as the pigeon (sound levels down to 0.5 Hz), and a few species produce vocalisations in the ultrasonic range (above about 20 kHz). As outlined in Chapter One, the experimental technique of playback is the standard way of investigating the meaning of vocalisations. Playback involves recording the vocalisations of a bird and then playing them back to another bird or group of birds and observing the results.

Sending a vocal message can of course take many different forms, as earlier chapters have shown. For birds (and many insects), which have such a high investment in communication by acoustic means, it is important to be aware that effective sending of messages may be impaired by factors in the environment in a number of ways.

We speak of auditory saturation, for instance, for sounds that are impossible to transmit over a long distance. Background wind, waves, rain, or movement of leaves in a forest may cause wave reflections and bring about a lowering of signal intelligibility and a diminution in the signal carrying power. Background noise of other species (e.g. insects and frogs) may also interfere with transmission of the vocal signal. Then there is aggregate noise produced by the same species living communally in a colony, in large family groups or a bachelor flock, and even background noise created by movement of wings. As you may have observed, hundreds of birds taking to the air at once can create a substantial noise even without vocalisation. All these factors may present difficulties in relaying a message.

The receiver must, therefore, be capable of extracting the relevant information from random background noise and have the capacity to detect information-carrying signals of an intensity which may be below that of the background noise. One cannot but be impressed when a penguin, for example, enters its colony of perhaps tens of thousands of other raucous birds and can detect and identify its young by sound alone.

A message, at its most basic level, reveals the species identity of the sender. The study of birdsong, for instance, makes it clear that each species has its species-specific vocalisations, although there may be individual variations, and even dialects according to region. Any vocalisation therefore at the very least conveys the meaning: 'I am here and I am a great tit' (or a starling, or a nightingale or any other species).

We distinguish broadly between the syntax and the semantics of a message. Syntax refers to the structure of the song or call. Semantics refers to the content or meaning of the message. The two can be intertwined. It is questionable in birds whether vocalisations are made without intending to impart meaning. The exceptions are a few cave-dwelling bird species such as the cave swiftlet (*Aerodramus vanikorensis*), which uses clicking sounds for echolocation just as bats do.

A bird's vocalisation may be simple or complex. But it is often misleading to claim that a vocalisation is 'simple', because our fleeting observations of one species may not represent that species' entire repertoire nor may we, as casual human observers, always be able to detect the finer distinctions in a vocalisation. For instance, it is now known that the allegedly 'simple song' of a finch has 13 themes and 187 variations. The entirety of vocalisation variations in birds is called a repertoire, just as in a human singer, and the number of different song types available to one species is referred to as the repertoire size. Repertoire size has been examined in quite a number of songbirds. From available information, it seems that the brown thrasher 'holds the record' in repertoire size, as Catchpole and Slater (1995) point out. The brown thrasher has an estimated repertoire size of between 1500 and 1900 song types. Improvisation and new learning may result in further changes and increases in the repertoire size. For instance, as J.R. Kirn and colleagues discovered in 1989, the red-winged blackbird adds to its repertoire each year.

But repertoire size, by itself, is not an indication of an increase in meaning. Here we must look for different parameters. Meaning is far more difficult to assess than repertoire size. We use the term 'vocabulary' to refer to the semantics—that is, the actual meaning of the calls. Passerines are said to have a vocabulary of about 20 different calls whereas gulls and other non-songbirds may have half that. However, research today is pushing back the limits further and further. For one of the most complex of songbirds, the Australian magpie, Kaplan has identified 37 distinct semantic units in the vocalisation so far. The number of variations has not been fully explored, although they appear to be in the hundreds for one specific bird alone. Given that individual differences are very marked in vocalisations of complex songbirds, we may expect a good deal of variation and with that variation may come complexity of meaning.

The understanding of meaning in avian vocalisation is in its infancy. Traditional ethology tended to describe animal behaviour in terms of four main motivational systems: aggression, fear, feeding and sex. These categories were related to physiological processes underlying the behaviour. In 1953 Tinbergen argued that behaviour was due to relatively invariant and immediate responses to internal and external stimuli. This approach was an important first step in studying vocal and other behaviours systematically. Since his ground-breaking work, much research has been undertaken to investigate the development of vocal behaviour in conjunction with physiological and even anatomical development.

More recent studies have shown that vocal behaviour in birds does not always conform to Tinbergen's simplified model. It is now known that learning plays a part in the development of song in all true songbirds (oscines) so far studied. There is a period of vocal plasticity—that is, a period during the development of the young bird when it is able to extend its vocabulary and learn its song. Even in those avian species with simple calls some learning may be involved. The period for learning may vary very widely between species. In some species of sparrow, learning is restricted to the first two months of life, while in others it may take much longer. Peter Slater of the University of St Andrews showed that the young chaffinch is able to learn new songs as late as ten months of age (Slater 1989). The vocalisations of Australian magpies remain highly plastic throughout the first year of life at least. Kaplan has found that hand-raised magpies are able to learn new sounds and new (human) words throughout this period. More details about learning to vocalise are given in Chapter Five. Here we want to emphasise that avian vocal behaviour is extremely complex and certainly not automatic or based simply on underlying physiological factors.

What is song for?

The functions that have been established for birdsong can be summarised as territorial defence and sexual attraction. Donald Kroodsma (1996) has argued that sedentary species may develop elaborate songs, whereas migratory birds may use song less for the purpose of advertising nesting or the transient territories. During the breeding season, the growth of male sexual organs may go hand in hand with changes in plumage (e.g. in the superb blue fairy wren), or with the onset of elaborate song for the purpose of attracting a female. Territorial defence by vocalisation is generally regarded as a more efficient way of communicating than physical confrontation. Less energy is expended in the process and injuries may also be minimalised. Many bird species first issue warning calls to an invader but then follow it by direct flight at the invading individual if the vocal warning was not sufficient to deter the invader. Neighbouring birds know their territorial borders and a form of truce, even if a watchful one, may exist between neighbours. This is illustrated by the white-throated sparrow (*Zonotrichia albicollis*) which sings far less energetically when a neighbouring bird approaches its territory than on the approach of a strange individual.

The connection between song and breeding is equally strong. There is ample evidence today that many males sing to attract a female just as some choose plumage to achieve the same result and some do both. Song requires energy and one of the arguments put forward is that prolonged and strenuous singing advertises the good health and fitness of a male, just as a shiny and colourful plumage may do so. Apart from its possible physiological function across a variety of songbirds, the communicative value of the song may be: 'Take me because I am healthy.' Further, the song may say 'I am experienced' and will therefore make a good partner. This comes about because song is acquired and perfection of tunes is a mark of a mature adult, with plenty of exposure to his species-specific calls.

Research in the 1960s has shown that auditory stimulation has a direct effect on the secretion of hormones that stimulate growth of the sexual organs and, in turn, stimulates the secretion of sex hormones. The secretion is induced by sound and, in some species, triggers the female to become ready for mating. A classic study by Daniel Lehrman (1965) showed that the cooing of the male dove triggers reproductive changes in the female.

Singing together

Duetting has been an important subfield of song study and it occurs in a wide range of avian species. It is now recognised that duetting plays an important role in the vocal communication system of birds, especially in the tropics. It is a specific form of communication in which one bird of a pair initiates a call and the other answers. It usually involves sequential calling rather than singing together, as used in human song. Duets may overlap but usually the calls of two birds follow each other so closely and so precisely that they sound like the vocalisations of one bird (see Figure 3.3). This is referred to as antiphonal song.

Although duetting may play a part in synchronising the gonadal state of the pair (to prepare for breeding), its functions also include communication when visual contact is lost or at risk of being lost. This is particularly true in

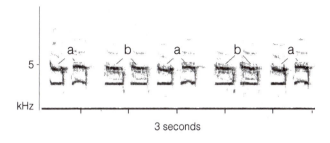

5 kHz

3 seconds

Figure 3.3 Antiphonal song of two magpie larks. Australian magpie larks (*Grallina cyanoleuca*) perform duets. In the spectrogram, because of the marked similarity of the vocalisations made by the two birds (a and b) and the precision of timing, it appears as if the vocalisations were made by just one bird. (Sound spectrogram by G. Kaplan)

wooded areas and dense rainforests (hence the prevalence of duetting in tropical regions) or during winter flocking and migration. Duetting may also occur to synchronise defence of a territory or, more commonly, to reinforce a pair-bond. Duetting seems to occur more frequently in pairs with a prolonged monogamous bond. Australian magpie larks (*Grallina cyanoleuca*) duet regularly (Figure 3.3), as do Australian magpies, the black-faced cuckoo shrike (*Coracina novaehollandiae*) and the bar-headed goose (*Anser indicus*), but the context in each of the duetting situations seems entirely different. Studies by Charles Blaich and colleagues (1996) found that pair-bonded zebra finches engage in contact-call duets far more frequently than unpaired finches, and in a non-random fashion. Duets are not necessarily initiated by the male. In the bar-headed goose or the bay wren (*Thryothorus nigricapillus*), for instance, it is the female who calls first, answered by the male.

Further distinctions of birds singing together are choruses and carolling. In the chorus, a whole group of birds sings at the same time. This may involve the countersinging of neighbouring and competing birds, or of

85

unrelated groups. There is a form of chorus that we call 'carolling' and this concerns a family group or communal breeders reconfirming their bond and, together, pronouncing their territory. Australian magpies and kookaburras (also called the 'laughing jackass') use carolling and countersinging to test the strength of a neighbouring group. As in individual calls, in carolling and chorus singing there may also be some status signalling involved. The parent bird will start the cacophany and then be joined by mate and offspring or helpers at the nest. In kookaburras (laughing and blue-winged), the offspring may supply a form of percussion support while the parent birds burst into full staccato calls ('laughing').

Variations of song

The loudness of a vocalisation (amplitude) can make a substantial difference to a message. Many bird species, as Richard Andrew of Sussex University has found, have loud–faint pairs of song display (Andrew 1961). The loud vocalisation may be for territorial display and can mean that the caller would attack if the territory borders were infringed. For instance, Carolina chickadees and Australian magpies have a vocalisation display that is uttered only when ready to attack. A fainter call signalled to mates and offspring may indicate that the communicator is ready to interact but not attack.

Thus, even if we consider only those vocalisations used for breeding and territoriality, the variations and richness of 'the message' can be substantial. Some species of gulls even have specific copulation calls. Among weaverbirds (songbirds of the subfamily *Ploceinae*), John Crook of Bristol University found that, in at least four species, females have specific vocalisations to solicit copulation (Crook 1969). In Australian magpies, females and males use the full song repertoire all year round. Bird vocalisations can also signal information about food; they can express anxiety or alarm, rivalry, attention or defence; they can indicate flying away (follow me) and similar short instructions. None of these may be specific to the sex of a bird. Male and females alike will utter calls in relation to predators and many other situations, but this depends on the context, as we saw in Chapter Two.

Attributing specific functions to birdsong is useful in ascertaining the meaning of the vocalisation and what evolutionary advantages might flow from one activity (song) over a host of possible others. However, seen only in an evolutionary sense, this approach may omit or underplay other aspects of song. To consider song only in terms of territory defence may underplay how it is learnt. Simply establishing a relationship between song type and territory may lead one to overlook, as Williams and Slater (1990) have pointed out, that both repertoire size and numbers of neighbours are likely to have strong influences on the distribution of song types in a population. They conclude that geographical variation of song may be an epiphenomenon of vocal learning (see Chapter Five) and one need not propose purposes for geographical variation in song or for song dialect boundaries.

Straightforward functional explanations of song may also be at a loss to account for a whole range of other vocalisations. For instance, one of the magpies that Kaplan raised spent a good part of the vocalising day running through elaborate variations of a long repertoire, for no apparent reason. The vocal pattern was rearranged every time and seemed to record the auditory events of the day, embellished perhaps, but recognisable as auditory events that had occurred within the bird's earshot. The bird was well fed and in a comfortable and relaxed posture when these extensive vocalisations were made. Free-ranging Australian magpies show the same behaviour at the height of summer, well before their breeding season and just after the worst pressures of feeding their young from the previous season are over, and the food supply is plentiful. These examples provide some evidence to suggest that singing may increase as the pressures of territorial defence and feeding of self and/or of the young decrease (quite opposite to the claim that singing increases purely for breeding and defence).

There may be 'cultural' aspects involved in singing at this time. For instance, magpie females may sing to their offspring while feeding them. This may not just include the individual song of the mother but also mimicked sequences. In one recorded case by Carrick, Robinson and Falls, made in the mid-1960s in Canberra, a magpie mother 'sang' something that sounded like a horse neighing to her offspring just prior to feeding them (original tapes acquired courtesy of Em. Prof. Bruce Falls). These mimicked vocalisations might belong to the cultural domain and may have no direct survival function, unless it can be argued that conveying the information of horses in the territory was vital knowledge for survival. Alternatively, it could have been a by-product of another form of mimicry that was vital for survival.

Meaning

Research on any aspect of semantics in the last 50 years or so differs from earlier studies in one exciting way. It is now known, and still being discovered in more bird species, that birds have what is called 'external referents' that result in referential signals. This means that they refer to objects outside themselves and communicate this to others. Studies in the 1950s, for instance, showed that some bird species signalled to conspecifics that they had found a specific food source. This was observed in herring gulls (*Larus argentatus*) by Frings (1956), and shown in a study by Friedman of the African honey-guide bird (*Indicator indicator*) which leads conspecifics to nests of wild honey bees (Friedman 1955).

The most common area of investigation of external referents concerns alarm calls. It has been shown for a number of bird species that the alarm calls for aerial predators are different from those for ground predators, as we saw in Chapter Two. In fact, Marler (1981) noted some years ago that warning calls about aerial predators have similar acoustic qualities among very different species of birds. Whether it be a chaffinch, a bluetit, a blackbird or a reed bunting (all European birds), the warning call is delivered with approximately similar intensity and at about the same pitch of 7 kHz.

The warning call is not easily located to its source. To explain this we have to digress briefly into the physics of sound. Hearing and locating a source is usually achieved by both ears (binaural); the ears assess and compare crucial elements of the message such as phase, intensity and time difference, thereby decoding the message and the location of the sender. Phase differences (referring to the timing of a sound wave reaching first one ear and then the other) can be detected more effectively at low frequencies. At higher frequencies wavelength decreases, rendering phase difference more difficult to detect, depending on the size of the predator's head, and hence the source more ambiguous. In fact, dependent on the distance apart of the listener's ears (and therefore the size of the listener's head) in each individual case, there is one frequency of sound that is impossible to detect using the difference in timing of arrival at each ear. Were this to be used as the frequency of the alarm call, the predator would be completely unable to use timing to locate the prey.

Identifying the location of the sound source is further aided by the so-called sound-shadow intensity effect. If, for example, the sound source is to the listener's right, the left ear will be in the 'sound shadow' of its head. An intensity difference thereby occurs between ears and this can help to establish the direction from which the sound comes. If a caller wants to avoid detection, the call would need to be pitched at a frequency that makes phase difference ambivalent and minimises the sound intensity effect. By doing so, the caller can avoid clear identification of direction of the call (hence the bird may call to warn of the presence of a predator without running an immediate risk of being caught by the predator).

Peter Marler (1955; 1981) showed that a call of about 7 kHz does exactly that and then showed that several species of birds use that frequency for alarm calling. This suggests that certain sets of alarm calls may become common to many species because of their physical properties. Discovery of such rules of communication also make it more understandable why communication between very different species is possible. Marler also found that alarm signals in some Corvidae and sparrows have similar structures and therefore induce interspecific reactions. In other words, the alarm call of one species may benefit a variety of other species, as we saw in Chapter One.

Many other signals used by avian species have not been fully investigated but some of them are certainly known to pet owners and those who rehabilitate wild animals. Among them are signals that indicate the presence of emotions. For instance, dogs have been known to cry for their owners. Birds shake in fear, accompanied by species-specific (often barely audible) high-frequency vocalisations. Animals communicate their emotions and desires to humans. Pets have also been observed to communicate with other species. Robert Leslie (1985) described a case of deception based on interspecies communication between two birds, a parakeet and a blue jay. The visiting parakeet, perched on the outside of the jay's cage, seemingly hungry, indicated by eye position and other cues that it wanted the chopped spinach in the cage. The blue jay moved the chopped spinach close to the edge of its cage, but on the inside, and when the parakeet reached for the spinach the blue jay delivered a sharp attack on the parakeet's head.

Attachment may be expressed by a combination of preening behaviour and low gutteral sounds. Birds make similar gutteral sounds when preening a partner. A similar low-frequency gutteral sound is emitted by Australian magpies when they preen a partner or offspring or the human carer. Our galah gives a specific short 'approval' call when asked whether he would like to come into the house. He follows this at once by descending from his outside perch and marching straight through the front doorway to his perch in the living room.

It is interesting to note here that similar patterns of intonation occur across human cultures. Anne Fernald, for instance, has shown that in humans melodious speaking signals approval, sharp, staccato bursts express disapproval or denial and low legato murmurs are for comforting—and this is common to different cultures (Fernald 1992). These patterns may apply not only to humans but to animal species as well. Sharp calls are usually interpreted as repudiating calls while low legato murmurs/purrs are associated with comforting: there is cross-species similarity as Marler (1981) described for alarm calling.

Mimicry

In birds, we have an additional group of vocalisations not equalled by any other group in the animal world, that of mimicry. Mimicry is extremely widespread and highly developed among Australian bird species and, less commonly, is found also throughout the rest of the world. The best known species for mimicry in the wild are lyrebirds (both species), Australian magpies and bowerbirds (several species). In contact with humans, even if remaining free, they can also mimic human speech. Among European birds, the starling is the star of mimicry. We know that parrots and budgerigars are excellent mimics in captivity but the first examples of mimicry in the wild have just been found recently, for example the African grey parrot (Cruickshank, Gautier et al. 1993).

The question remains: what is mimicry for? Why would birds deliberately transgress their species-specific sounds and move into the vocal territory of other species? We know that insects can mimic appearance, smells and even light signals, and dolphins and seals may use some vocal mimicry, but as far as we know today only birds mimic other species extensively in vocalisation (more on this in Chapter Five). Purists argue that such mimicry by birds is not 'true' mimicry; they define 'true' mimicry as having deceptive purposes useful for survival (more in Chapter Five).

Taking the models from studies of the insect world, true mimicry involves three parties: the true identity of the mimicked one, say butterfly A, the mimicker, called butterfly B, and the predator that is fooled by butterfly B (i.e. the predator will not eat it because it looks like the unpalatable butterfly A). There has been no unambiguous evidence to date that birds mimic to avoid predation. However, it is possible that a bird may mimic another to safeguard a territory. While this is not predation, such mimicry would have clear survival function either in safeguarding a territory from a predator using a similar food chain as the species defending its territory, or by repelling a predator who may consider preying on the young in the nest. We must also take into account differences between intentional and unintentional mimicry, as considered in Chapter Two for signalling in general (see the 1997 review by Christopher Evans for more detailed consideration).

A second reason for mimicry, and the one most commonly cited, is related to the breeding season. Lyrebirds, for instance, adorn their songs during the breeding season with all manner of sounds, taken from the sound repertoire available to the male. This typically includes mimicry of other birds, the most distinctive being currawongs, kookaburras, yellow-tailed black cockatoos and catbirds (mostly species that mimic others themselves). Lyrebirds may also include sounds of barking dogs, car horns, creaking door hinges and even chainsaws, all sound segments that will then liberally spice their own species-specific calls. It appears that lyrebirds sing their long sequences of mimicked calls to attract the female. It is as if they 'wear' the song component like medals—the more elaborate and extensive the collection, the more the female is impressed.

But the function of vocal mimicry may extend even further, at least in the case of the Australian magpie. Kaplan has recorded all the vocalisations of hand-raised Australian magpies and found that they mimic sounds very selectively.

Extensive exposure to some sounds resulted in no mimicry while very short exposure to others immediately produced mimicry. The vocal capabilities of one female juvenile bird were such that it would have been possible for her to incorporate the sounds made by those species she chose not to mimic. There was, for instance, a visiting butcherbird that sang very near her aviary and did so repeatedly over several days until it eventually disappeared. This bird was never mimicked. However, kookaburras housed next to her aviary were mimicked after she heard their distinctive 'laugh' just once and then only for less than a minute (see Figure 3.4). The kookaburras had suffered injury and had

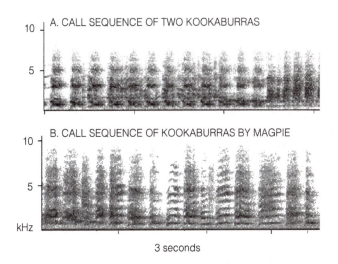

Figure 3.4   Mimicry of kookaburra by a magpie. A. A sound spectrogram of two kookaburras (*Dacelo gigas*) laughing together. B. Mimicry of the kookaburra's laughing by an Australian magpie (*Gymnorhina tibicen*). Note the matching rhythmic pattern. The fundamental notes also match but most of the overtones do not—the magpie's rendition of 'kookaburra' is rhythmically very precise but it is a little more melodious than the original, demonstrating the vocal differences between song (passerine) and non-song (non-passerine) birds. (Sound spectrograms by G. Kaplan)

been in an aviary next to the magpie for several months. Once the kookaburras' health improved, they began to vocalise. The kookaburras were therefore familiar to the magpies, but their vocalisations were not because there are no free-ranging kookaburras in the area. Within a year, a pattern emerged: all sound-producing species, including humans, who belonged permanently in the magpie's wider 'territory' (visible range of the aviary) were mimicked while temporary visitors, such as the butcherbird, were not.

In this specific case it seems possible to argue that territorial knowledge is very important for a species that is highly territorial, and was incorporated into the magpie's own repertoire. The sonogram in Figure 3.4 shows that the mimicry of the kookaburra is more melodious than the original, but the magpie has attempted to follow the rhythmic patterns of the 'laugh' rather precisely, mimicking not just one kookaburra but the joint calls of two birds.

The quality and complexity of bird vocalisations has also raised the issue of whether some bird species may be capable of communication that approximates aspects of language. First, it needs to be noted that 'communication' and 'language' are two different concepts. We have already seen that effective communication is possible by means other than sounds and language. Second, there is the issue of how we define language. Well-known contemporary linguists such as Steven Pinker (*The Language Instinct* 1994) and Derek Bickerton (*Language and Species* 1990) have made a strong case for species-specificity of human language. They argue so on the grounds that human languages are qualitatively different in structure from systems of animal communication. We have no problem with defining human language as 'species-specific'—that is, to argue that human language has attributes found exclusively in humans just as there are attributes unique to other non-human species. There is a problem, however, when researchers derive from this the view that an absence of language (already argued to be unique to humans) is then said to be a flaw in animals. This is circular reasoning. What is reasserted, and often only in an implied fashion, is not just the uniqueness of human language but the processes required to achieve language—that is, intelligence.

There have now been several studies that have challenged the correctness of the view that human language is unique. For instance, a study of Japanese quails undertaken by Keith Kluender, Randy Diehl and others at the University of Texas showed that quails can learn phonetic categories (Kluender et al. 1987). These results challenge theories of speech sound classification that posit uniquely human capacities (more of this in Chapter Six). Irene Pepperberg has shown that Alex, the African grey parrot, understands commands and concepts and can communicate them. Phonetically and semantically, there is then evidence that not all processes associated with the acquisition of human language are unique to humans.

Conclusion

Avian species have certainly developed great virtuosity in both vocal and visual communication. For this reason alone human fascination with birds will continue to be strong. It is clear from research so far that some, if not all, of the signals made by birds are not only emitted reflexively, but involve learning and quite complex decision making, depending on social context. Some of the astounding vocal abilities that certain bird species share with mammals are almost certainly the outcome of parallel evolution, meaning that these abilities evolved separately in the avian and mammalian lines of evolution. Other special features of bird communication probably existed in vertebrates, long before mammals evolved and used them. Irrespective of their evolutionary origins, the vocalisations of birds follow principles or rules that are relevant to other species. As Saito and Maekawa (1993) and many other researchers have pointed out, avian vocal communication, when compared to human vocal communication, can be most instructive.

CHAPTER FOUR

COMMUNICATION IN MAMMALS

There has been less well-controlled experimental research on the communication systems of mammals than on those of birds. Most recent research on mammals has found that their communication systems are more complex than was once thought, and that many of these signals vary according to the context. As in other species (see Chapter Two), some signals are sent unintentionally and reveal something of which the sender is not aware, whereas others appear to be sent intentionally.

Sending a visual message

The visual signals used by mammals are diverse and complex but there are basic signals that strongly resemble each other across many mammalian species, including humans, and some of them appear to have been used over long stretches of evolutionary time. Visual signalling in mammals is usually confined to posturing of the body, such as stretching, jumping, arching the back or limb use. Tool use purely for visual signalling does occur in mammals, but is relatively uncommon.

In Chapter Three, reference was made to the bower of the bowerbird in its courtship displays and we pointed out how visual displays may involve use of objects other than the body. Such use of objects in visual displays is of importance in avian communication, and there are even examples of fish, amphibian and reptilian species using objects for display. It is therefore important that, among mammals, we do not often find the use of objects to enhance visual displays. One of the few examples cited in the literature is that of John MacKinnon (1974), who observed wild orang-utans. When he kept following them through the rainforest, they looked down from the trees and started to throw sticks. Some of these 'weapons' barely missed him and, in a few cases, stick throwing became more intense when he continued to follow the orang-utans. MacKinnon rightly read this as a warning signal that he should stay away. Another exception may be the gibbon's branch shaking which some (e.g. Peter Marler and Richard Tenaza) have not regarded as an auditory signal. Baboons throw stones at predators.

Visual displays may be subdivided according to the use of discrete regions of the body. The body as a whole, including posture and movement of the body, can have signal function. Locomotion itself is a form of communication. A variety of different gaits and the corresponding body postures may well determine how another animal will respond. Limb movement is a separate aspect of visual display.

For mammalian species with tails, the tail may be used extensively to accentuate the meaning of the animal's emotions or intent, or it may even be a signal on its own. In many ungulates and carnivores the tail is used in greeting, threats and courtship, each with its own postures and speed of movement. Monkeys also use the tail extensively in friendly and aggressive displays (see Figure 4.1, which includes tail and genital display), as outlined by Richard Andrew (1972) of Sussex University. In Chapter One we referred to the use of tails by lemurs in 'stink fights': raising of the tails and waving them so that odour is wafted towards the other animals. We did not mention the visual aspects of this display: the long tail of *Lemur catta* is striped black and white. In moonlight this would be visible and may be an aspect of the signalling in addition to the odour. In many species, the tail mirrors the head movement in several

97

Figure 4.1 Genital display of marmosets. The marmoset on the left is displaying its genital region to a human who is outside the cage. This posture is a threat. Note that the marmoset's ear tufts are raised and its mouth is closed (compare to Figure 4.3C). At the same time as displaying its genitals, the marmoset is looking at the target of its aggression. (Photograph by University of New England Media Unit)

displays. For instance, holding the head and tail high signals high arousal and/or dominance. Lowering of head and tail signals submission and even fear. We return to this in Chapter Six. Familiar body movements in our own human signalling system are shared with many other mammalian species (e.g. waving, head shaking, jumping, raising the arms).

A third region of the body from which signals can emanate is the face (Figures 4.2 and 4.3). Most of the

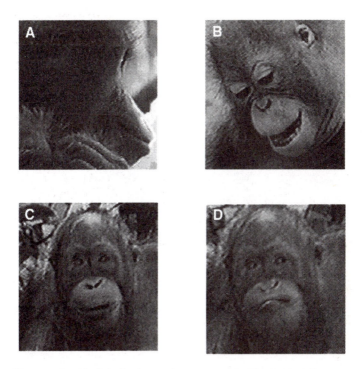

Figure 4.2 Facial displays of orang-utans. These are Bornean orang-utans (*Pongo pygmaeus*), which we filmed in Sabah, East Malaysia. A. Jessica is holding her one-week-old baby and smiling, just as a human might. B. A play face—the lips are puffed, the mouth is partly open and only the lower teeth are showing (compare to the play-threat display in Figure 1.5, in which the mouth is opened wide and both the upper and lower teeth are displayed). C and D. Video images, taken in close succession. The young male is expressing mild anger, first by parting the lips to grunt (C), and then by pouting his lips (D). (From videotapes by G. Kaplan)

research on faces has been carried out on primates and this is a very large field of investigation. Facial expressions and non-verbal communication in primates have been of interest partly because a primate's face is similar in anatomy

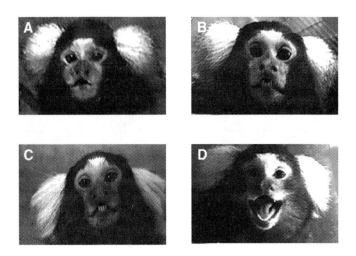

Figure 4.3 Facial displays of marmosets. These images of the common marmoset (*Callithrix jacchus*) have been taken from videotaped recordings. A. The contact facial expression which accompanies the twitter call (see Figure 4.4). B. Expression of apprehension or of mild fear and threat. Note that the mouth is drawn back and the lower front teeth are displayed. When a human makes a facial expression like this in the presence of marmosets, they become very agitated. C. Expression of a higher level of fear compared to B. The mouth is similar to that in B but the ear tufts are lowered. C. The highest level of fear/threat is expressed and the marmoset is making the tsik call (see Figure 4.4). The mouth is opened wide to display all of the lower teeth and the incisors of the upper jaw. The ear tufts are pulled back. (Video images courtesy of M. Hook-Costigan)

to the human face and partly because Darwin singled out the face as an important site for the expression of emotions (see Chevalier-Skolnikoff or Ekman for details).

Early work by Jan van Hooff (1967) from the University of Utrecht, Netherlands, showed that there are possible primate homologues of both human laughter and smiling. The vocalised or near silent bared-teeth display has been described as phylogenetically one of the oldest facial expressions, shared as it is not just by primates and humans but by many other mammals as well. Usually this gesture is associated with a threat or strongly aversive stimulation. A silent bared-teeth display is a sign of fear and submission, found in many higher primates. Our human smiling may have undergone a change in meaning although there are bared-teeth displays in primates that do express friendliness. By contrast, van Hooff thought that laughter had different phylogenetic roots from smiling. Laughter is associated with breathing and breathing technique—that is, a vocal activity—while smile is related to facial muscular movement only. Chimpanzee laughter is closely coupled with breathing, but Robert Provine (1996a) of the University of Maryland in Baltimore found that, unlike humans who exhale continuously during the act of repeating laughter, chimpanzees produce one laugh sound per expiration and inspiration. Signe Preuschoft's study of Barbary macaques (*Macaca sylvanus*) further confirmed the phylogenetic difference between the smile and laughter made by van Hooff 25 years earlier (Preuschoft 1992).

Another facial expression found in many species, as well as in humans, is the yawn. In mammals yawning is probably more widespread than has been described in the literature. When humans yawn it usually means that the yawning person is tired or bored, as a detailed study by Robert Provine confirmed (Provine 1996b). Yawning is thought to be 'contagious', like laughter, and it can also be sent as a signal to express disapproval. In mammals, yawning may mean a variety of things. In baboon parlance, a yawn by itself either means uncertainty or expresses fear which can turn into a signal of aggression when other body posture signals are given. By contrast, our dogs yawn when they have been praised! Or yawning may be an expression of frustration.

Facial expressions that we share with primates are grimacing, tongue movement, staring, certain eye movements and expressions of sadness. In particular, the eyes play a role in facial expressions that humans share with primates. The eyes, often used with other facial expressions, can express fearfulness, anger, curiosity and real or feigned indifference. The stare, as J.-P. and A. Gautier (1977) described it, has several meanings as used by Old World monkeys. One is a threat. Another is a reprimand. A male gorilla will use a stare if grunts are unsuccessful in settling squabbles between females or juveniles. A stare, in dogs, can also express a wish or demand. Dogs 'stare us down' when they beg from humans or each other. When our dogs are reprimanded for begging, their entire erect body posture disappears at once and the head is turned away.

Juichi Yamagiwa (1992) from Kyoto University points out that the role of stares in primates is rather complex and may have different context functions among bonobos than among rhesus macaques or gorillas. Bonobos and chimpanzees may use mutual staring as a form of positive contact with each other, while the stare of the gorilla without any subsequent physical contact may be used in conflict resolutions. In the late 1950s Niko Tinbergen suggested that displays of any kind can be conveniently divided into those that are distance-increasing and those that are distance-decreasing. Peter Marler (1968) extended this classification by suggesting that primate communication functioned to achieve either aggregation or dispersal. Moreover, as observed in bonobos, a direct stare may be a means of seeking a sexual encounter or it may be a reprimand or assertion of dominance.

Eye stares in primates are often accompanied by lowering of the eyelids. The eyelids then become exposed and, in primates, can be rather spectacular. In various macaques they are white and in some baboon species a silvery colour. As they remain exposed or flashed, the signal is made more threatening or at least more conspicuous. The human habit of painting the eyelids for accentuation is an interesting custom in view of primate signalling with the eyelids. Raising the eyebrows either by retraction of the scalp or independent eyebrow movement further reveals the eyelids. J.-P. and A. Gautier (1977) point out that in various mangabeys and baboon species scalp movement is accentuated by side whiskers or the presence of toupees which can be raised or flattened.

There is also a furtive expression used by humans and orang-utans when they want to look at something they ought not to. An extension of this kind of eye movement is the flirt. Our own work on eye movements in orang-utans has shown that eye movement is employed more often than head movement. We have also observed 'flirting' orangutans who edged closer and closer to each other and only occasionally looked at each other from the corner of their eyes. These eye movements were so brief that they were not detectable by our naked eye but had to be discovered in frame-by-frame analysis of video material. Additional signals that we, as a species, have largely lost, such as lip smacking, ear flattening, eyelid flashing and hair bristling, are common in most primates. Tragically for monkeys and apes, their very physical expressiveness has made them desired 'objects' for display in circuses, clubs and other entertainment centres. Group living, which is partly responsible for an extensive range of physical signals, makes them interesting animals to observe and their signals, even if often misunderstood, have a familiar touch for the human species.

The reason for the perceived similarity of visual signals given by the body and especially by the face between humans, monkeys and apes lies not only in the morphology of the face but in associated brain mechanisms. In humans, the left side of the face is dominant in emotional expression. In Marc Hauser's study of the facial expressions of rhesus monkeys and the human response to their expressions, he found that facial expressions in rhesus monkeys begin earlier on the left side of the face and involve larger movements of the facial features than on the right side of the face (Hauser 1993). Thus the left side of the face is more expressive. This has to do with the control of such expressions by the brain. The right hemisphere of the brain controls the left side of the face and the right hemisphere is involved with emotional expression in a range of species.

By contrast, the left hemisphere of primates and other species processes species-specific calls. In fact, human and non-human primates have the same pattern of brain asymmetry for sending and receiving signals. Alan Fridlund (1994) has recently warned, however, that we should not jump to the conclusion that commonalities necessarily mean a shared genetic heritage. We could be dealing here with analogies, the result of convergent evolution.

Using sound signals

Mammals frequently use sound for communication, sometimes within the hearing range of humans but also outside it. The range of frequencies used outside human hearing may be below (infrasound) or above (ultrasound) the thresholds of human auditory perception.

Echolocation

Use of ultrasound by animals was discovered this century. This was largely the result of work by H. Hartridge in 1920 and G.W. Pierce from Harvard University. Hartridge worked on bats and concluded that they were able to avoid objects in flight by listening to the echo of their own sounds in ultrasonic range. Pierce took up entomology as a hobby and later wrote about ultrasonic sound in crickets.

This discovery of the use of ultrasonic sound for navigation and communication was more important than we might think today. It opened our minds to the possibility that our own senses may not suffice for a full understanding of animal communication. Human audition ranges from about 0.02 kHz (20 cycles per second) to a maximum of about 20 kHz (20 000 cycles per second). The most sensitive and comfortable hearing for humans lies at frequencies around 2 kHz. As we have seen already, this frequency range is also commonly used by birds. We now know that, as well as a range of insects—from moths to grasshoppers, crickets and locusts—there are rodents, whales, dolphins, seals, sealions and certain primates whose vocalising and hearing range extends well above that of the human species. John Altringham (1996) of the University of Leeds explained that some bats of the Megachiroptera family use echolocation but all bats from the suborder Microchiroptera, involving literally hundreds of species in Old and New World areas, use echolocation, whether they are omnivorous, insectivorous or carnivorous.

Echolocation is not used just for detecting objects (to be avoided in flight) or potential prey but may be used for conspecific location as well. For instance, between birth and weaning the pups of the Mexican free-tailed bat (*Tadarida brasiliensis mexicana*) live in segregated colonies or 'creches' of about 4000 pups per square metre. Each female has a single offspring and needs to locate it, usually twice in a 24-hour period. Gary McCracken (1993) established that a mother finds her pup largely by locational cues resulting from echolocation.

The discovery of echolocation in sea-dwelling mammals, such as dolphins and whales (cetaceans), was made as late as the 1950s by A.F. McBride and W.N. Kellogg (Kellogg 1961). They found that the echo-ranging signals (clicks) are highly directional and can be employed over a large underwater terrain. The sonar characteristics of sea mammals all differ and have their own structures and frequency ranges. Transient killer whales, for instance, use short and irregular echolocation 'trains' composed of clicks that appear to be structurally variable and low in intensity. Even within the same species of killer whales (*Orcinus orca*), there are substantial differences in the echolocation pulses. Whales who are resident in a region use regular sequences while those of transient killer whales are irregular. As Lance Barrett-Lennard (1996) and his colleagues argue, sequences of short-duration sounds that are irregular in timing and frequency more closely resemble random noise than do sequences of more structured sounds and thus are less likely to be detected by marine mammals (the prey of killer whales) against background noise. By using these 'noisier' sounds to locate their prey, killer whales can detect and approach marine mammals without their knowing.

Signals as reliable as those used in echolocation can also serve a communicatory function. In the Microchiroptera there is evidence for a continuum between the use of ultrasound for echolocation and for communication. It has been shown by Fenton (1994) and many others that the echolocation calls of one individual can be used simultaneously by others, both conspecifics and other species. For example, the 'feeding buzzes', which are echolocation calls with high-rate repetition rates produced by bats when they attack airborne targets, indicate that prey is available and are often exploited by conspecific bats to identify vulnerable prey. Some moths also use 'feeding buzzes' to detect the presence of predatory bats.

Yet echolocation does not necessarily give the killer whale a substantial advantage in catching prey, as Lance Barrett-Lennard and his colleagues (1996) found. Although most fish species have auditory sensitivity in the low-frequency range of around 3 kHz and are thus unlikely to detect killer whale clicks, the typical prey of the killer whales can in fact hear the clicks. The pinniped (seals) and cetacean (dolphins, whales) prey of transient killer whales have acute hearing up to frequencies beyond 30 kHz, well within the range of killer whale sonar clicks. Porpoises swim away from killer whales at high speeds on erratic courses. Dolphins and grey whales move into shallow water when killer whales are nearby. Some prey have also adapted by placing their own echolocation signals outside the range of killer whale hearing. For instance, killer whales cannot hear the echolocation pulses of Dall's porpoises, which centre on frequencies of 135–149 kHz, because killer whales can sense frequencies only up to about 105 kHz. However, killer whale hearing can detect the sounds generated when porpoises surface and breathe and so they may find this particular prey without the aid of echolocation signals. Transient killer whales often search for prey in waters close to the shore. Here, there is camouflaging noise from waves striking the shore. Signalling over a noisy background was discussed in Chapter One.

From whistles to roars

Other sounds that sea mammals make cannot be catalogued here—there are too many. Like birds, their vocalisations are species-specific and often each individual has a characteristic pattern of vocalisation. In the last 40 years there has been a great expansion of our knowledge of vocalisations in sea mammals. By the 1960s, considerable knowledge of the complexities of vocalisations of sea mammals had been acquired and Roger Payne had described the vocalisations of humpback whales as song. This reached popular consciousness (there was a best-selling recording called 'The Songs of the Humpback Whales').

We now know that dolphins, for example, possess richly diversified whistles, usually at lower frequencies. We know that, like birds, their vocalisations contain acoustic signatures of individuals and there are many sounds with precise meaning. M.C. and D.K. Caldwell (1965) first reported in the 1960s that bottlenosed dolphins (*Tursiops truncatus*) had individually specific signature whistles. And a study by Janik, Dehnhardt and Todt (1994) found that, beyond individual identities, the whistles also contain context-related information. As in birds, different alarm calls are given to refer to different predatory species, such as sharks, human beings or killer whales. Perhaps the most spectacular dolphin behaviour is their response to distress whistles made by other dolphins. A distress call by a sick or injured dolphin will bring the others to its rescue. Also, dolphins have lungs and breathe air so they need to raise their heads above the surface of the water at regular intervals; baby dolphins must do this at intervals as short as two minutes. William Stebbins (1983) has reported that a dolphin having difficulty in rising to the surface to take air will be assisted by other dolphins and literally lifted up to the surface. Agonistic behaviours are expressed by jaw clapping or arching of the back. The tail flukes, the flippers and the tail itself may be employed in such displays and, when accompanied by rising and falling whistles, may indicate strong threats.

Seals have long been used in circuses because of their playfulness and ability to learn tricks. Seals, sealions and walruses (all pinnipeds) were, until recently, thought to command only a very limited range of vocalisations confined to land. A study in 1984 by Evelyn Hanggi and Ronald Schusterman of harbour seals (*Phoca vitulina*) found that they also vocalise under water during the breeding season. The vocalisations are different for each individual. Some of their vocalisations during the breeding season, such as the roar, are combined with visual aquatic displays. It has been suggested that this either plays a part in male–male competition or is a way of attracting females. Male walruses produce bell-like sounds which they use in combination with visual displays to attract females. However, it is perhaps a little premature to draw conclusions on the function and meaning of these display behaviours and the roars of seals. It has been known since the 1980s that seals may mimic but usually when they are on land. This aspect is covered in Chapter Five.

Vocal signalling and reproduction

Seasons of the year, determining the reproductive cycle, are accompanied by classes of vocalisations with characteristics specific to the context. Many mammalian species have developed elaborate strategies surrounding the time of reproduction. Vocal, visual or chemical signalling during the ovulatory period (or breeding readiness of the female) occurs in most mammalian species.

These signals function in a social context where it might be prudent for the female to advertise her reproductive condition or, in other cases, to hide the onset of the periovulatory period. Females may exploit their readiness for mating to entice males to fight on their behalf, or to ensure that the best possible male can be found. In elephant seals (*Mirounga angustirostris*) the female gives a copulation call which incites aggressive competition between males. She witnesses the fight and the winner mates with her.

The mating strategies used in baboon societies are very different. The threat of infanticide is very real in baboon troops and it occurs particularly in troops where only one male is present. An outsider male who successfully challenges the position of the troop male will attempt to kill offspring that are not his. Groups with several males are thought to be safer, partly because of the mating strategies employed by the female. Females call during mating and, as O'Connell and Cowlishaw suggest (1994), these calls may invite several males to mate with her, thereby creating uncertainty about paternity. This uncertainty might well protect her offspring. Baboon females also signal their oestrous period by the reddened skin of the buttocks, which they display to males.

We know from other mammals that vocalisations may stimulate ovulation by the female. For instance, the roars of male red deer (*Cervus elaphus*) are said to trigger copulation readiness, if not ovulation, in females. Red deer males roar loudly and repeatedly during the breeding season. In a study by Karen McComb (1991), the roaring rate was found to be positively associated with reproductive success and fighting ability. The energy metabolism and call intensity, duration and rate may serve to advertise fitness in males. Although roars often precede fights with competing males, McComb found that male deer roar in the same way whether competitors are present or not and go on roaring at a rate of two roars per minute throughout a 24-hour period. These vocal displays are accompanied by horn and broad-side displays. She found that females preferred males with a high roaring rate whether the males fought or not.

Vocalising in primates

The second largest group of mammals in which vocalisation has been examined and analysed in great detail is the primates. Humans and most anthropoid primates have sacrificed high-frequency sensitivity for improved auditory discrimination within a more restricted frequency range. They have finer discriminatory powers in all three parameters of vocalisation (frequency, intensity and timing, i.e. temporal disparity) in the lower frequency range. However, marmosets and tamarins are known to hear ultrasonic frequencies as well as the range audible to humans. Figure 4.4 shows vocalisations of marmosets within the human auditory range.

Most primates are gregarious and this has led researchers to argue that the communication systems of such species are more complex, in line with the complexity of their social organisation. The squirrel monkey (*Saimiri oerstedi*) from Costa Rica has become the most common laboratory model for studies of primate vocalisations over the past 20 years, especially calls expressing emotions and isolation. Most of these studies have been conducted in the artificial context of a laboratory supplemented only occasionally by studies in the natural environment. Laboratory work is important for controlled studies but field work is needed to confirm what is found in the laboratory. One of the few field studies was undertaken by Sue Boinski in 1991. She found that, in the squirrel monkeys' natural environment, the duration of peep vocalisation (contact calls) is positively correlated with spatial separation, confirming that the duration of their peep calls provides information about the distance of the caller.

Some of the long-range vocalisations of primates are specialised calls that primates use on discovering food. Call characteristics are influenced by the quality of food, its quantity and divisibility, as found also in birds. Marc Hauser (1993) and colleagues at the University of California, Davis, found that chimpanzees use a vocalisation, which the researchers called a 'rough grunt', in the context of finding large amounts of food. The interesting aspect of such vocalisations is that it shows an individual is capable of making several decisions before vocalising, such as: 'Is there

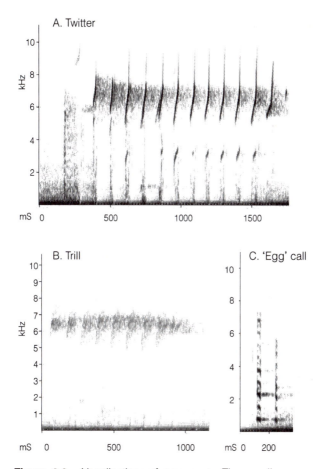

Figure 4.4   Vocalisations of marmosets. These calls were made by captive common marmosets (*Callithrix jacchus*) in our colony at the University of New England. A. Twitter calls, which are given for social contact (see Figure 4.3A for the accompanying facial expression). Note the steep change in frequency. These calls extend into the ultrasonic range but the high frequencies are not represented in the figure. B. Trill call, given when the marmoset is slightly aroused. C. Crackle or 'egg' call, which indicates mild alarm. These are just some of the vocalisations produced by marmosets. For more details see Epple 1968. (Recordings by M. Hook-Costigan)

more food than I need?' and 'Can this food be divided among others without a fight?'

Habitat acoustics influence the structure of vocal signals by primates, as they do in all species. Charles Brown (1995) and colleagues, of the University of South Alabama and Purdue University, found that the rainforest is less favourable for high-fidelity sound propagation than open spaces but, nevertheless, species that live in that environment have managed to evolve vocalisations with high-fidelity transmission by using the right frequency and other acoustic aspects. Tropical rainforests, in particular, pose several problems for effective communication that are not found in savannas and open woodlands. The forest is an environment with high background noise, largely caused by insects, and high reflection of sounds from trunks and leaves. Foliage, temperature gradients and ground effects can also contribute to fast degradation of the structure of a signal. However, alternative methods of long-distance communication are not really available (trees and leaves also obstruct visual contact) and so forest-dwelling species have to use vocalisations for contact calling. Brown and colleagues have shown that selection for vocalisations with reduced chance of distortion has influenced the form of the vocal repertoire of two rainforest species (the blue monkeys, *Cercopithecus mitis*, and grey-cheeked mangabeys, *Cercocebus albigena*), more strongly than those of two savanna species (vervet monkeys *Cercopithecus aethiops*, and the yellow baboon, *Papio cynocephalus*). The forest environment leads to adaptation which overcomes problems of distortion and thus influences the form of signal repertoires.

In rainforests individuals lose sight of each other and must rely on acoustic signals to stay in touch whereas savanna monkeys can usually retain visual contact with each other. This might explain other aspects of the evolution of vocal repertoires with different physical characteristics in primates living in rainforest versus savanna. Mangabeys and baboons have choruses, just like birds, enlisting many individuals to participate. They scream and, although their vocalisations are very similar, the distortion scores are lower for the forest-dwelling mangabeys than for the savanna-based baboons.

The habitat of the New World squirrel monkeys is also densely foliaged so in this species, too, there is a real possibility of the separation of the troop. Boinski (1991) noted that the female vocal exchange among squirrel monkeys acts as an 'auditory beacon' to monitor the position of females and hence of the troop. To verify this, common marmosets were experimentally tested for responses to loss of visual contact. An experiment that deprived common marmosets (also arboreal monkeys of the South American rainforest) of other sensory contacts showed that they immediately modulated their calls in duration, peak frequency, frequency range and median frequency. Lars Schrader and Dietmar Todt (1993) found that modulation increased with decreasing sensory information about mates. Also, the amplitude of the mammals' calls increased as much as 8 decibels during the experiment, a technique that improves transmission of calls. They concluded that modification of specific call parameters can protect information encoded in the calls against possible signal disturbances caused by the environment. Thus call modulation is found to be linked to spacing.

Most of the auditory signals of the forest species studied so far have been classified as messages related to the integration of the whole group, such as alarm calls or contact solicitations, but such calls, of course, are not limited to forest dwellers. Alarm calls may relay information about the type of threat that is imminent (i.e. signal what kind of predator is approaching). The semantic content of vervet monkey alarm calls was shown in important work by Seyfarth and Cheney (1980) and described in detail in Chapter Two. Their experiments revealed that the vervet monkeys classify and 'read' the message purely on the basis of the acoustic structure, even when deprived of any visual clues. They found that vervet monkeys achieve major changes in signal function by changing frequency peak—

calls with an early peak serve an integrative or cohesive function for the group; calls with a late peak indicate a state of arousal (sexual or agonistic).

Larger forest-dwelling primates have succeeded in exploiting vocalisation over long distances, despite the severe constraints imposed by a forest environment. Mangabeys in the Kibale Forest in western Uganda can be heard (by the human listener) from a distance of 500–600 metres through dense forests and, at certain times, even from as far away as 1200 metres. The loud calls of chimpanzees, known as 'pant-hoots', are also audible for more than 900 metres, as Waser (1977) and colleagues have reported. The 'long call' made by orang-utan males, a spine-chilling roar, is audible for at least one kilometre.

Gibbons (*Hylobates* sp.), also forest dwellers, are among the most conspicuous vocalisers of all primates. They are territorial and monogamous. Not unlike some bird species, they sing duets in which the female usually takes the lead. These are extensive vocalisations and the skill involved in producing them lies mainly in the coordination of the 'song' in duet. The song of gibbons also tells of the length of the pair relationship—inexperienced pairs usually have problems with their duetting coordination and may not finish their song. Their sounds can be heard for miles across the rainforests of South East Asia. In this case, the song is less concerned with maintaining contact with individuals than with protecting territory (i.e. advertising their presence in a patch of forest).

Nonvocal sounds

Sound signals are not confined to vocalisations. Mammals may be better equipped to make sounds with limbs than birds (see Chapter Three). And there is plenty of evidence that the limbs are used extensively in a large variety of contexts, such as territorial defence, courtship and identity marking. For instance, the banner-tailed kangaroo rats (*Dipodomys spectabilis*) use individually distinct foot-drumming

114

signatures to communicate individual identity to territorial neighbours (Chapter One). They can also discriminate the foot-drumming signatures of neighbours and strangers. Jan Randall (1994) thought that familiarity among neighbours promotes a stable social organisation in this solitary, nocturnal rodent. Foot drumming is also used in the threat displays of noctural prosimians. Gibbons shake branches, break them off and drop them in what has been called a 'brachiation' display. It is a stunning and very noisy affair, achieved solely by using branches. Alpha male chimpanzees (i.e. the dominant males) like to make noise too when they display, breaking branches and bashing them as they run. Presumably the noise reinforces perception of their physical strength. Gorillas use chest beating, first documented in detail by G.B. Schaller in 1963. Lip smacking is another nonvocal sound that plays an important role in some apes and monkey species during allo-grooming (grooming other individuals). It is used by an approaching monkey to indicate its peaceful intention and then maintained during the process of allo-grooming.

Earlier research on primates attempted to catalogue primate vocalisations, particularly those of the great apes (chimpanzees, gorillas and orang-utans). The vocalisations of orang-utans have not been studied systematically, however, but studies on chimpanzees and gorillas have had some interesting results. When Marler and Tenaza compared the vocalisations of gorillas and chimpanzees in 1977 they found that 'the most striking conclusion to be drawn from the data is . . . the surprising degree of correspondence between the two species in the rank order of use of corresponding calls'. By this they mean that there were important similarities between the species in the order of most used to least used vocalisations. This is an important point because the social organisation of chimpanzees is not at all like that of gorillas. This finding may indicate their common evolutionary origins, cultural transmission by learning or the fact that both species are subject to similar environmental constraints on vocal transmission. Almost certainly all three factors have an influence.

Scent deposits and olfactory markers

Chemical communication is a widespread form of communication among mammals. It has been recorded in rodents (mice, hamsters, rats, voles), marsupials (koalas, sugar gliders, opossums), ungulates (horses, deer), dogs, primates (Old and New World monkeys) and even in elephants. Chemical communication is much older than mammalian existence. Fishes, amphibians and reptiles also use chemical communication, in alarm signals and in courtship, in kin recognition and territorial defence. The most ancient marsupial family, the Didelphidae (e.g. the grey opossum), shows extensive scent-marking behaviour. They also show oestrous synchrony, caused by odours known as pheromones, and oestrous activation, also triggered by pheromones. The latter led Barbara Fadem (1985) to the conclusion that olfactory communication has a long evolutionary history. The scent-releasing glands of many species are larger in the male, they are more highly developed during the breeding season and largest at sexual maturity. Species with well-developed scent glands tend to be polygynous and territorial males tend to scent-mark more than non-territorial males. We have seen that communication tends to become more complex with the complexity of the group, and territoriality is another variable that adds to the range of communicative needs. Territoriality needs to be communicated and hence scent-marking becomes a constant activity in the quest to maintain a territory.

Chemical signals seem to occur most frequently among species that are subject to predation and have a limited home range. In primates, at least, it is known that the most developed system of chemical signalling and communication is found in those species most subject to predation, especially those that are nocturnal and/or arboreal. Such species include New World monkeys (e.g. marmosets and tamarins) as well as Old World nocturnal species (e.g. prosimians). All these species rub their scent glands on objects in their environment, marking them with their scent (see below and also Chapter One). Prosimians also mark themselves with urine: they urinate onto their hands and rub it into the fur.

Primate species that are terrestrial (living on the ground) and diurnal (active during the day) tend to rely on chemical signals to a lesser degree. For instance, apes do not have well-developed olfactory lobes and do not rely on scent-marking. Apes are large and/or live in strong groups and generally have few predators. They are mobile and may forage over large areas. This has led to the belief that intense reliance on olfactory signals occurs in species lower on the evolutionary scale and that use of olfactory signals has been largely superseded over time to include other senses considered to be more suitable for communication. However, apes do rely on olfaction to signal reproductive conditions and olfaction may play a greater role in other aspects of their social behaviour than we currently realise.

The line between intentional and unintentional communication by odours may be fluid. For instance, individual A (female) of a species may give off scents that will entice individual B (male) to mate with her. Individual A may not have produced the olfactory signal intentionally, it being merely a result of her changed hormonal state. Individual B has learnt to interpret the signal correctly. But let us say that individual B has the choice of several females who are emitting signals similar to those of individual A. Individual B can therefore choose according to quality and type of smell. This is referred to as mate choice. Whether the choice is made intentionally or unintentionally is likely to vary with the species. As we saw in Chapter Three, males of many species, avian and mammalian alike, have developed most elaborate strategies to ensure they will succeed in getting a mate. Olfactory, visual and vocal communication is used to achieve this end. Moreover, mate choice is not confined to males. In many species females do the choosing and the male the displaying and competing.

Scent may be used for territorial claims and defence and requires more than merely releasing a specific odour from the animal's body. There is a good deal of work involved in scent-marking a territory. Gisela Epple, of the Monell Chemical Senses Center at the University of Pennsylvania, found in the 1970s that olfactory signals have a complex set of communicative functions in the life of the common marmoset. Marmosets have several glands that release different odours, under the chin, on the chest and in the anogenital region. First, there is intragroup communication, including sexual communication, regulating social relationships among adults and infant–adult relationships. Second, olfactory signals are important in intergroup communication concerned with territorial defence and the formation of new groups. Third, olfactory signals help to maintain orientation in the environment. Further studies by Epple (1988) and colleagues on saddleback tamarins (*Saguinus fuscicollis*) and cotton-top tamarins (*Saguinus oedipus oedipus*) have shown that their olfactory communication may fulfill a similar range of communicatory functions as in the marmoset.

While olfactory signals in the urine play an important but balanced role in some monkey species, other mammals depend on olfactory cues almost exclusively. For instance, interactions between house mice depend to a significant extent on olfactory communication. An experiment conducted by Jane Hurst (1993) and colleagues, at the University of Nottingham, showed that male house mice remain tolerant towards subordinate males largely on the basis of urine marking in spots and streaks across the entire territory (substrate odour deposits). Resident male mice, both dominant and subordinate, behave aggressively towards subordinate males without their fresh odours to the group's home territory. It is obviously important to be known in an olfactory capacity to dominant males. Urine quality in subordinate males is different from that of dominant males.

Hurst and colleagues suggest that regular urine markings by subordinate males is an efficient system, allowing territorial males to concentrate their defence on intruders. It appears that mice and quite a number of other mammalian species need to supplement their visual displays with cues from other sensory modalities, in this case smell. The substrate marking by a subordinate male reassures the dominant male that no attack is planned on his status and territory.

In the European rabbit (*Oryctolagus*), chin marking is one of the most conspicuous forms of olfactory communication. Robyn Hudson and Thomas Vodermayer (1992) found that these chin-gland secretions served sexual advertisement by females but also non-sexual functions. Female rabbits are able to discriminate between chin marks from different animals according to the donor's hormonal state. The researchers conclude that chin marking may also play a role in the establishment and maintenance of group identity. Group stability and territorial stability may thus be served by extensive use of olfactory signals. Michael Stoddart (1992) of the University of New England has found similar use of odours in the social behaviour of marsupial sugar gliders (*Petaurus breviceps*).

We have not yet raised the possibility that signals may get lost, misread or overlooked. The issue of selective attention and selective memory may be of great importance in communication and a study in its own right. Suffice it to say here that a recent study on golden hamsters (*Mesocricetus auratus*) by Robert Johnston (1995) and colleagues has drawn our attention to the fact that not all messages have a recipient and that, for some species, this seems to have evolved by design. The researchers tested hamsters for their responses to the partially overlapping scents of two individuals and asked whether the tested hamsters would be able to identify both individuals. They found that the hamsters remembered only the scent mark on top—that is, the one deposited most recently—even if the other scent had been identified before in a separate test. If scents are 'read' only selectively, according to a process of masking, there may be important outcomes for us in the way we think of communication as part of a process of selective detection and selective perception.

The sense of touch: tactile signals

A good deal of communication can also happen by touch. Grooming in mammals is an important gesture of intimacy and closeness. It reinforces pair-bonding, as it does in birds, and in certain primate groups, such as rhesus monkeys and baboons, grooming is associated with status within the group. Dominant members of the group are groomed by subordinate ones. Sometimes, there are lines of animals each grooming the next one in the row. Tactile communication in baboons and bonobos (pygmy chimpanzees) is often used for appeasement, reassurance and expressions of loyalty. An animal's intention to groom usually has to be advertised so that the individual being approached is assured of the peaceful purpose. In baboon groups, the approaching individual will smack its lips loudly and then continue the lip smacking throughout the grooming process.

Another form of body contact is embracing. Obviously this form of tactile contact relies on the existence of limbs that can do the embracing. We find this form of communication largely in monkeys and apes, although it does occur in mating frogs and toads. Hugging, cuddling, cradling are activities not just confined to mother–infant interaction but are found among non-related animals, even of adult age. Bonobos may be unusual, even among apes, in that they use 'loving' tactile contact (all manner of tactile activities, including sexual) for settling conflicts within the group. Notably, as Frans de Waal and Frans Lanting (1997) point out, it is mostly the females who maintain peace by means of physical contact with each other. Lip touching of two conspecifics (i.e. kissing) may be simply a friendly greeting or it may be used as an overture to sexual advances.

Orang-utans, too, use touching extensively in certain

social contents. First, mother–infant relationships, which are very intense and long-lasting, are established by close physical contact (as we describe in detail in our book *Orang-utans in Borneo*, 1994). Juveniles and even adults (usually females) continue to use touch as a form of communication, often without eye contact. This touching behaviour was shown in their association with us when we were observing free-ranging rehabilitating orang-utans in Sepilok, East Malaysia. One orang-utan juvenile who had taken a particular liking to Gisela Kaplan came out of the rainforest on a subsequent visit. She took Gisela's hands, turned them gently palm upwards, looked at them and then slowly and deliberately ran her index finger along the lines on the palms. Juveniles will often walk along holding hands. Although orang-utans are largely solitary, rather than living in groups like the other apes, the sense of touch in personal relationships continues to play a role through adult life. It obviously features in sexual behaviour.

Elephants use their trunks extensively to communicate with each other. They have very sensitive skin and the trunk needs only to glide gently over the body, or touch the trunk of another, for a message to be conveyed. The trunk is used to help baby elephants to stand up and walk when the herd is moving to new feeding grounds, and also for reassurance and many other subtle communications.

Dolphins and whales use touch as a form of communication for many of the same reasons (as far as we know) that touching is used in other species. They nuzzle each other with the snout or swim alongside each other, brushing along the skin.

Many mammalian species use licking as a form of reassurance, as an expression of bonding or a signal of status. Dogs and related canids, for instance, use licking extensively and in a variety of social contexts, as Michael Fox (1971) first showed and reported in his book on canid behaviour. Dogs go through extensive daily rituals of reassuring each other and of reconfirming the status of the lead bitch. Our own dogs do this by touching each other's nose or licking the other's snout. Conflict resolution is usually swift, whether it is fierce or friendly. In the wild, a dog may be expelled from the pack or even killed (depending on the species). Our dogs, three Rhodesian ridgebacks, siblings from the same litter, two females and one male, will usually resolve conflicts in a conciliatory manner. In conflict resolution, licking is directed behind the ear, on the neck and, if allowed, the anogenital region. Small bites, shoves and pushes are all part of a gentle and friendly communication. Hence, tactile communication is widespread among a large variety of species.

Recognition of individuals

Can animals recognise conspecifics as individuals? Do they relate to individuals in a specific way? Or do they just respond to key markers of categories, such as plumage colour, a particular scent or a specific vocalisation, that are sufficient to trigger 'familiarity' or 'stranger' status? In the mechanistic view of animals, the latter would certainly be regarded as sufficient for survival. And are such questions meaningfully applied to all animals or only to some? Stanley Cohen (1994) specifically draws attention to the intelligence and capabilities of pet dogs (see also Fox 1971). Most pet owners are convinced that their pet can identify them as individuals. This recognition of the owner is part of the close relationship that is formed between owners and pets (see Chapter Seven). But to what extent does this recognition of individuals apply in the wild, and how do animals achieve this? It is not always easy to scientifically determine what signals might be used to achieve recognition of individuals.

For animals to recognise the individual conspecifics as unique entities, it is assumed that they would need to have memory of each individual, a representation composed of a variety of key markers, or 'integrated, multi-factor representations'. This assumption was tested in golden hamsters (*Mesocricetus auratus*) by Robert Johnston and Paula

Jernigan of Cornell University, who showed that golden hamsters respond to individually distinctive signals on the basis of the meaning (or the referent) of the signal. Male golden hamsters were exposed repeatedly to scents of females in oestrus. These experiments were designed to show that the males distinguished clearly between a familiar female (an individual) and a strange one, and that they could distinguish between two odours of the same female but attribute them to the one individual. They suggest that this result indicates the importance of higher-order, cognitive processing in the social behaviour and communication of hamsters because the animals categorised stimuli according to their significance and not strictly by their sensory characteristics (Johnston & Jernigan 1994).

Recognition of the alarm calls of different conspecifics also seems to be important because some individuals signal the presence of predators more reliably than others. Unreliable signallers that 'cry wolf' too often (see p. 45) could be ignored if they are recognised. Some recent research on the ground squirrel (*Spermophilus richardsonii*) has shown that this may be the case. James Hare of Brandon University in Canada recorded the alarm calls of different squirrels and then played them back to selected individuals in their natural environment (Hare 1998). He found that the squirrel no longer attended to hearing the same individual's alarm call after it had been played back four times. Habituation had occurred. Then he played back either another alarm call by the same individual or the alarm call of another individual. The squirrel became more vigilant after hearing the call of the new individual but not after hearing another call by the first individual. It was able to distinguish one individual's call from another's.

To be able to make distinctions between individuals would also be useful in observing rules in established social hierarchies and in other social relationships in group-living animals. For example, individual recognition in rhesus monkeys has been shown to be very sophisticated. Vocalisations by a dominant member of a group may

require a different response than vocalisations by a subordinate. Maintenance of group structure and (in the case of
alarm calls) even survival may depend on this. Habituation
to alarm calls by trusted/senior individuals of a group could
threaten survival.

Receivers of calls do not just distinguish individuals but
they can respond to the calls according to the caller's
relationship to themselves. In a social system in which
the mother's relatives (matrilineal line) are important,
categorisation of their calls by lineage might be important.
Playback experiments using calls of unrelated and related
individuals have been conducted by Drew Rendall and
colleagues (1996). They have shown that female rhesus
monkeys (*Macaca mulatta*) respond significantly faster and
longer to contact calls of matrilineal relatives than to
calls from other relatives and non-relatives. Their study
demonstrates that rhesus monkeys are able to distinguish
unrelated individuals from kin. Even after such experiments
under controlled conditions, it is not certain whether true
recognition of individuals has occurred because other cues
(such as the location of the individual) may assist in the
identification of an individual. The researchers point out,
however, that the capacity for vocal recognition of individuals and kin represents an important adaptation in
long-living primates with complex social relationships between individuals.

As we have seen before in the discussion by Janik,
Dehnhardt and Todt (1994), dolphins use signature whistles
that identify individuals. There seems little doubt that
mammals recognise each other individually but exactly how
they do so in each species requires much more research.

Communicating with primates

The idea of humans communicating effectively with primates via language or a system of symbols has generated
much innovative research. The genetic closeness of the great
apes to humans seems to make it possible to devise ways

of bridging the gap between animals and humans. If real communication with the great apes could be achieved, the pot of gold at the end would be information about their unobservable personality: their thoughts, memories, wishes, fears and a host of other things that could not be deduced from observation alone or that are not unambiguously measurable. Some notable researchers have tried to create that bridge by including apes into their personal lives, raising chimpanzees and gorillas as if they were their own children. Others have moved into the natural environment of the apes, staying in close proximity to them until they were finally tolerated or even accepted by the group. These pioneering research efforts led to a sense that some real communication had taken place, based on trust and mutual respect. Many new insights were gained in the process and, if we can speak today of awareness and consciousness in animals, this is largely due to the research on communication undertaken with great apes.

However, researchers have followed a number of blind allies. For instance, much of the interest in vocal abilities in primates was generated by the wish to understand the origin of human language rather than animal communication. Lewin (1991) argues that chimpanzees may hold the only key to the origin of the human language. These studies have centred on the superiority of vocal communication—instead vocal communication may not be a superior form of communication, simply the one we understand best and one that has served the evolution of human primates extremely well. Also, it is often assumed that species closer to humans (i.e. primates) should show more evidence of vocal learning (i.e. higher plasticity in their development) than species that are more distant from us in evolutionary terms. This is not the case. Development of vocalisation and vocal learning has been shown to exist in songbirds (as we will discuss further in Chapter Five). In fact, overall, less is known about vocal development in primates than in birds, even though we now have some very detailed knowledge of the vocal communication systems of the great apes. Attempts to teach apes to speak have failed while, as we have already shown, there have been very successful attempts to teach birds to speak. This is because the vocal apparatus of apes is not constructed to produce human speech sounds. Apes can communicate with humans using sign language or symbols, as discussed in Chapter One.

Ethical questions in communication research and conclusion

Human curiosity about animal learning, adaptation and communication has often involved ignoring the animal as a whole organism, especially when only one aspect of the animal's behaviour may be of interest in a particular study. Meredith West and her colleagues (1997) at Indiana University have recently raised ethical questions in relation to experiments on vocal learning in birds and primates. They argue that researchers, in their desire to establish parameters of learning, have often accepted methods of testing that would now be unacceptable. Some early experiments, for instance, saw monkeys raised in very small chambers for one year with no physical access to other animals. Similar ethical issues have arisen for the study of birdsong where prolonged isolation has been used to control the experiment (we refer to this again in Chapter Five).

Although conditions for animals have improved greatly over the past 20 years, living conditions for experimental animals inevitably involve deprivations. Most experimental species are kept in sterile environments and confined to cages where they have little to do. These problems, ethical and experimental, have of course been recognised and many studies have attempted to remedy the situation by improving the physical environment of captive animals and/or by complementing laboratory studies with field studies. The problem is that there is no perfect system of studying animal communication that is completely non-invasive, involves no deprivation and is scientifically unassailable. In the natural environment, controls are more difficult to establish and hence results may be more unreliable. The laboratory, on the other hand, while providing opportunity for controls, may distort results by its very artificiality. Meredith West and her colleagues found that differences in social and physical settings in cage and aviary tests could lead to different levels of competence (or the lack thereof) in social and communicative skills.

The matter of learning and communicative competence invites further comment and this will be taken up in the next chapter. Suffice it to say, there appear to be many aspects of communication with a long evolutionary history which we share with birds and mammals alike, be this in body postures and displays, in facial expressions or in certain vocalisations involving alarm, reassurance and anger. It is these that we have tended to recognise most readily and that are being catalogued. The challenge is to recognise the complexities of species-specific forms of communication with which we have less in common.

CHAPTER FIVE

LEARNING TO COMMUNICATE

In earlier chapters we have discussed some of the varied patterns of communication used by different species. In most cases we referred to the communication patterns of adults—very often these patterns are not present in the behavioural repertoire of infants or juveniles but develop as the animal grows up. This development is partly due to maturation involving the expression of different aspects of the genetic program (which is read out from the genes passed on from generation to generation) as the individual gets older, and partly due to experience and learning. These processes are often regarded as separate, but they are not. At every stage of development, maturation, experience and learning interact.

Let us consider a familiar example that is very relevant to communication. The maturation of the reproductive organs and the consequent release of sex hormones has a major impact on vocal communication in many species because the hormones affect the growth of certain parts of the brain and the vocal apparatus—the larynx in mammals and the syrinx in birds. In the human male changes in the larynx cause the voice to deepen. In birds, syrinx growth often coincides with the age at which new vocalisations emerge. For example, roosters start to crow when they approach sexual maturity because this is the time when their sex hormone levels rise. If the sex hormone, testosterone, is injected into young chicks they will crow, although they sound like very squeaky roosters because the syrinx has not yet developed enough to make a full crowing sound.

In songbirds, it is known that the sex hormones affect the development of certain structures in the brain that are used to control singing: as Fernando Nottebohm (1989) of Rockefeller University has shown in his research on the canary (*Serinus canarius*), certain regions of the forebrain enlarge as the amount of testosterone circulating in the blood increases. The genetic program for development plays a part in determining this sexual maturation process but experiential influences from the environment also interact.

To continue with the songbird as an example, the season of the year provides the trigger for the development of the sexual glands. As spring approaches, the length of each day increases and this is the stimulus that causes enlargement of the sex glands and increased release of sex hormones into the bloodstream. In males, this in turn causes the regions in the brain that are used for singing to enlarge. Once this has occurred, the bird is able to sing its special breeding season songs.

In establishing the canaries' song, learning is also involved. Male canaries elaborate on their songs each year; they learn from hearing themselves and other canaries, and they remember their own song from year to year. Thus, the song that the bird produces has been determined by the interactive effects of its genetic program, the experience of changing day length, the level of sex hormone, and learning. Genes and environment have important and completely interacting roles in determining the song of each canary and, as might be expected, each individual sings a different song. We discuss this interaction in more detail in Chapter Six. Here we note that there are differences between species in when they sing and whether only males sing. As said before, both male and female Australian magpies sing and they do so all year round. So far, there has been little research of widely divergent species.

Not only must a bird know how to sing, but it must also know in exactly what place and at what time of day it would be advisable to sing (singing in another bird's territory would provoke attack). The bird must also know to which individual its singing should be directed. Similar criteria apply to all species and also to other forms of communication. As communication is social behaviour, it is not surprising that there are many different aspects of communication that have to be learnt. First, we discuss learning to produce vocalisations and then we consider the importance of learning when, where and how often to communicate.

Song development in birds

There has been much interest in the study of song development in birds. Three kinds of evidence indicate that a vocalisation is learnt. The first kind of evidence is the development of abnormal vocalisations in birds that are raised in isolation from other members of their species, so that they never hear the vocalisations of their own species. The second is the abnormal development of vocalisations in individual birds that have been deafened in early life. This is not a procedure that we support on ethical grounds, and it is unlikely to gain approval for experimentation today, but it was used three decades ago and we report the results because they add valuable information that should neither be lost nor repeated. The third kind of evidence is that of vocal imitation or mimicry of the vocalisations of other species and of sounds in the environment.

There is no evidence that vocal learning occurs in the Galliformes (chickens, turkeys, quails, pheasants) or the Columbiformes (pigeons) but it does occur in the Passeriformes (in the large number of different species of songbirds, known as oscines, but not in absolutely all the Passerines), Apodiformes (hummingbirds) and Psittaciformes (parrots). There are, of course, numerous species in each of these categories. The ability of parrots to imitate human speech, and sounds such as creaking doors and bottles opening, is well known (see discussion on the parrot Alex in Chapters Two and Three and also a 1975 paper by Dietmar Todt), but many songbirds also mimic sounds in their environment and, when hand-reared, will mimic human speech. We discussed this special kind of learning in detail in Chapter Three—here, we are more concerned with the first and second kinds of evidence showing that avian vocalisations are learnt.

Learning of vocalisations is characteristic of those oscines that have complex songs as well as those with local dialects (variations in their vocalisations from one region to another). One of the latter species is the chaffinch (*Fringilla coelebs*). Some time ago, William Thorpe, of the University of Cambridge, conducted some most important experiments in which he hand-reared male chaffinches in isolation away from other members of their species and then looked at their song development. In this species it is only the male that sings, due to the presence of testosterone in the males. When the chaffinches became adults, the songs of the hand-reared males were very different from the songs of wild, adult chaffinches, although they were of roughly the same length, covered roughly the same range of frequencies (pitches) and were subdivided into packets of sound in somewhat the same way. It was as if the males reared in isolation retained a template for the song but, lacking social experience with their own kind, they were unable to learn the species-specific song (Thorpe 1961).

As confirmation of the importance of learning, it was found that, if the male chaffinches are played a tape recording of a chaffinch song as they grow up, they learn that song and produce a song that is almost identical. The same has been shown in other species, such as the song sparrow (*Melospiza melodia*). Other species show a similar dependence on hearing another bird singing in early life but, unlike the chaffinch, they need to interact with a living bird—simply hearing a tape recording of the sound is not sufficient. The Australian zebra finch (*Taeniopygia guttata*) is an example, as we discuss below.

Even establishment of the template of the song requires

some learning but, in this case, the bird learns by hearing itself. This was first demonstrated in the song sparrow by deafening birds early in life. The deafened birds developed songs that were entirely different from the songs of adults in the wild. They had either no evidence of a template of the species-specific song or a very crude template, much less structured than the template that develops in isolated, hand-reared song sparrows. This means that their song was even more abnormal than that of hand-reared members of their species. The same result was found in deafened chaffinches and other songbirds.

Learning to sing occurs very early in life. Certain vocalisations are learnt more readily than others: each species selects to memorise particular vocal patterns. Genes seem to determine this initial selection of the first memories of song (see Marler 1991 and 1997 for more detail). Later learning shapes further selection of memories for song development.

There are several distinct phases in the development of song, as we will illustrate by discussing the chaffinch. Soon after hatching, young chaffinches produce begging calls to which the parents respond by supplying them with food. By the time of fledging (at about five weeks old), these calls have been replaced by rambling, soft vocalisations, referred to as 'subsong'. Subsong is often produced when the birds are dozing or perching quietly. The bird runs through a whole series of different notes and the sequence can be very long. Subsong occurs in many species and, as Peter Marler (1970) has pointed out, it has a remarkable similarity to the babbling sounds that human infants make when they are acquiring speech. Both the subsong of birds and the babbling of humans provide auditory feedback—the individual hears the sounds that it is making—and so this is probably a stage at which self-learning occurs. The equivalent of subsong also occurs in parrots during a stage of life when they are practising their learnt vocalisations. Irene Pepperberg (1991) has reported on what she calls 'solitary sound play' made by the parrot Alex when he was being taught new vocalisations. At these times, Alex produced sounds that were similar to, but not exactly the same as, the new words that he was learning.

Subsong of the chaffinch's comes to imitate parts of the parents' song, although not precisely. The latter song is called 'plastic song' because it is still variable and not yet that of the adult. The bird's song practice subsides during the winter. Next spring singing begins again and this time it is subsong interspersed with plastic song. One month later, the song crystallises into 'full song'. The same pattern occurs in many other species of songbird, including song sparrows, cardinals and buntings. The Australian magpie does not follow this linear pattern of song development to crystallised song, although it does have a plastic song.

As mentioned above, chaffinches exposed to an adult's song during early development learn that particular song and produce a copy of it when they themselves are adults. This exposure to the adult's song need occur only during the first few weeks of life; the bird will then reproduce that song in adulthood even without further exposure to it for many months. This shows that there is a sensitive period in the chaffinch's early life during which song learning occurs. In chaffinches, and in many other songbirds including zebra finches, song is learnt early in life and then, once they become adults, they do not change their song again. Canaries also learn their songs in early life but they are able to change their songs from season to season when they are adults. It appears that they go on learning throughout their lives.

Nor is learning in adulthood limited to canaries: some parrots have been reported to learn new sounds when very old. We acquired a parrot (a galah) of more than 60 years of age and he learnt new words after moving into our household. These words were the names of two of our dogs (Julie and Luke) which he calls out when the dogs misbehave. Not only has he learnt to imitate the words but he knows they refer to the dogs and a specific situation—he has never used the words out of context and he does not use them very often. This ability to change vocalisations in later life also appears to apply to the natural vocalisations of parrots.

The same ability has been shown in budgerigars by Susan Farabaugh and colleagues at the University of Maryland. These researchers found that individual caged budgerigars (*Melopsittacus undulatus*) shifted their contact calls so that they resembled more closely those of another budgerigar caged alongside. The budgerigars showed mutual learning of each other's calls. By imitating each other, they converged their calls so that they became more alike (Farabaugh et al. 1994).

The ability to continue to learn in adult life does not, however, lessen the importance of a sensitive period for vocal learning in early life. There appears to be a window that opens in early life and allows the bird to learn a wider variety of songs than either before or after that sensitive period. This was demonstrated clearly by experiments conducted by Donald Kroodsma in the late 1970s (Kroodsma 1978). He exposed long-billed marsh wrens to a large number of different songs, a few songs every three days. The period of exposure began soon after hatching and continued until about 85 days of age. The wrens learnt very few of the songs they heard before about 25 days of age, although the number they learnt increased from ten days of age on. The best period for acquiring a variety of songs was 25–55 days after hatching but there was a low period around 40–45 days; from 55–80 days there was a decline in the number of songs learnt, although the exposure to different songs was just as various throughout this entire period of time. The results show clearly that there is a sensitive period during which the marsh wren learns new songs (Figure 5.1).

The ending of the sensitive period may depend on changing hormone levels; an injection of testosterone into zebra finches before the normal end of the sensitive period has been shown to curtail the learning of new songs. This contrasts with the onset of song production in the next

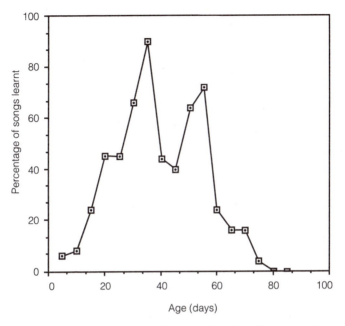

Figure 5.1   Sensitive period for song learning. The percentage of songs learnt by long-billed marsh wrens (*Cistothorus palustris*) at different ages after hatching. Over each three days, the birds were exposed to a few song types. Different selections of song types were played every three days until the birds had been exposed to a large number of song types over a ninety-day period. As the graph shows, the birds copied more of the songs heard between days 25 and 55 than at any other time, although somewhat fewer songs were learnt between days 40 and 45 than at the peak times. (Calculated from the data of D. Kroodsma presented in Slater & Jones 1997; the values presented are only approximate)

spring season when testosterone levels rise and the zebra finch sings the songs it learnt earlier during the sensitive period. It would appear that high levels of the hormone testosterone crystallise the song so that no new learning will occur. The same hormonal condition also stimulates the singing of the songs that have been learnt already. In adults the seasonally fluctuating levels of testosterone also affect song: a recent study by Troy Smith, John Wingfield and colleagues at the University of Washington has found that male song sparrows sing songs that are more variable in the autumn, when their testosterone levels are low, than in spring, when the levels are high, although the same repertoire of songs is sung in both seasons (Smith et al. 1997).

Sensitive periods for learning are not restricted to song learning or to avian species. There are sensitive periods for learning other behaviours, such as a sensitive period for forming social attachments by the process of imprinting. There may also be a sensitive period for learning language in humans, as isolated examples indicate but do not prove. There is the documented case of Genie, a human child who was denied any form of normal social or linguistic experience for the first 13 years of her life (reported by Curtiss and colleagues at the University of California, 1974). Genie never acquired full speech capacity but the abnormality of her first 13 years, and indeed the years that followed, may have contributed to this failure of recovery. There have been similar cases with comparable results but all these cases of isolated humans have had highly abnormal aspects that confound the conclusions that can be deduced. This might also be said of the birds that were reared in isolation. It is not possible simply to take something away—in this case, the bird's normal experience of hearing song and other social interactions—without having unexpected effects on behaviour in general. The process of development is not a simple equation from which one can extract something without untoward effects.

The inability to learn song or language after an early life of social deprivation might be an aberrant outcome not directly related to the simple subtraction of a normal aspect of social experience. There is a well-known example that may help to illustrate this, and that is the experiments performed by John Paul Scott (see Scott & Fuller 1965), in which he raised dogs in isolation from the time of their birth. When they were brought into contact with people at a later time, they behaved in very abnormal ways, one of which was to rush and bite at the flame of a cigarette lighter. Being raised in isolation did not lead just to an absence of some patterns of behaviour but to the emergence of behaviours never seen before. These results alert us to adopt caution in the interpretation we give to experiments in which animals are raised in social isolation, as in the studies of the songbirds.

Singing tutors

We have said that chaffinches and marsh wrens will learn songs from tape recordings played to them during the sensitive period. This is not the case for zebra finches and some other species. They need to see and interact with another bird of their own species at the same time that they hear it singing. Even if the other bird sings within their earshot but is hidden from their view behind a screen, they will not learn their species-specific song. It is some aspect of interaction with the singing bird that counts, as shown by Patrice Adret (1993), who was then at the University of St Andrews. He was able to train zebra finches to sing by allowing each bird, caged alone, to peck at a key to turn on a tape recording of a zebra finch's song. By turning on the tape recorder in this way the birds were able to interact with the artificial 'tutor'. The birds trained in this way would peck at the key many times in a day in order to hear a small segment of song (only 15 seconds) and they often flew up and down in front of the loudspeaker as the tape recording was playing. They learnt to sing the same song as the tutor and produced it when they became adults. Control birds exposed to the same tape recordings of song but in a passive way (they could not turn it on themselves) did not copy the recorded song. This shows that some form of interaction with the tutor is essential for learning to occur, no matter how unusual that interaction is.

Peter Slater and colleagues at the University of St Andrews have shown that a zebra finch may prefer to learn the song of its own father, but this is not at all a straightforward process (Mann & Slater 1994). Male zebra finches usually learn their songs in the second month of life. In the experiments conducted by Slater, the young zebra finches were housed with their parents until they were 35 days old, and so each could hear its father's song over this period, which precedes the sensitive period for song learning. Then each young bird was caged separately in the central part of a cage with three partitions (Figure 5.2). From day 35 to day 100 of life each bird was exposed to singing birds placed in the cages on either side. In the first experiment, an adult male was housed alone on one side and an established pair of birds on the other side. Neither male was the parent of the young bird in the central cage. The young birds learnt to copy the song of either the single or the paired male, although, overall, there was a tendency for the paired male's song to be preferred over the single male's song.

The next experiment exposed the young zebra finch to its father caged alone on one side and its mother with an unfamiliar and unrelated male in the cage on the other side. Of the 13 birds tested in this way, ten copied the song of the unfamiliar male housed with the mother, two learnt their father's song and one learnt equally from both tutors. Thus the chosen tutor is the male paired with the bird's mother, not the actual father, even though the father's song had been heard for the first 35 days of the bird's life.

The final experiment gave the young zebra finch a choice of learning from its father housed with an unfamiliar female on one side, or from an unfamiliar male housed with its mother on the other side. Of the 16 birds tested, ten learnt to copy their fathers and six copied the unrelated tutor. In this case a preference for the father's song is shown. This preference could have been established by the young bird's exposure to its father's song from hatching until day 35. However, the preference to copy the father's song after exposure during the sensitive period for song learning is not straightforward, because it occurs only when

138

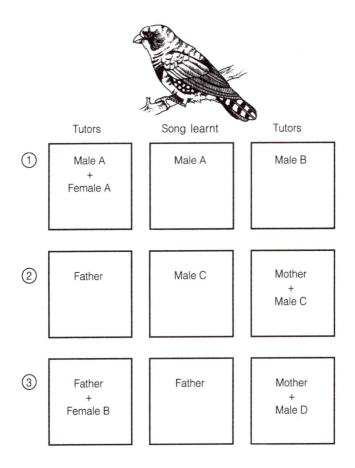

Figure 5.2 Choosing a song tutor. Each young male zebra finch was placed in a central cage with potential song tutors on either side. The song copied by the learner is indicated in the central box. Males A to D and females A and B are unrelated and unknown to the learner. Note that the learner has a preference to learn the song of a male paired with a female (1) and also for the song of his father (3). The song of an unfamiliar, unrelated paired male is preferred over that of the father, if the father is not paired (2). (This figure summarises the results of Mann and Slater (1994))

the father has a partner. If he is unpaired, the mother's partner is preferred over the father. Hence both mother and father influence the bird's selection of a tutor.

Preference for a particular singing tutor is, as these experiments have shown, a rather complex business. Another experiment found that tutors that are more aggressive and interact with the young zebra finch by pecking and chasing it are copied more than less aggressive ones (Weary & Krebs 1987). We assume this is because even aggression increases the interaction between the tutor and the young bird that is learning, but it is surprising that a somewhat punitive interaction would be effective. This is an area that deserves further investigation.

The bond between mother and offspring is not unimportant in the learning of song. Research by Meredith West and Andrew King (1988) on the North American cowbird (*Molothrus ater*) shows that the female can be most important in shaping the song of young males in this species also. As this species is parasitic—that is, it lays its eggs in the nests of other species, as cuckoos do—the young are raised without hearing the calls of their own species. Instead, after fledging, they form flocks in which singing by the males is shaped by the young females. The female performs a display of 'wing stroking' when she is attracted by the song of a young male. This apparently reinforces the male because he is more likely to sing the same song again if the female has performed this display. Therefore, in time, the songs of the males become matched to the preferences of the females. The females train the males to sing the correct song even though they do not sing themselves. If the males are put into a flock with females of a different subspecies of cowbird, they learn, also in response to the females wing stroking, to sing the song of that subspecies instead of their own.

The cultural transmission of song

The transmission of song from one generation of an avian species to the next by the process of learning has been seen by ethologists as cultural transmission. In fact, several researchers in the field (e.g. Slater & Ince 1986, and Trainer 1989) refer to the changes in song that result over time as the song is passed from generation to generation as 'cultural evolution', as distinct from genetic evolution, which we discuss in Chapter Six. It is thought, however, that the changes that occur as song is passed on are due to errors in copying (i.e. learning produces a song that is not an exact copy of the song that the bird heard) rather than being innovations on the part of the singer or some new form of adaptive behaviour. It is inevitable that small errors will creep into the copied song over time but, nevertheless, copying is surprisingly accurate, as we describe above. In addition to this source of change in the song over time, variations also result because each bird may copy elements of songs from more than one other individual.

The amount of change in the song from generation to generation varies with each species of bird. Peter Slater and his colleagues (1980) have estimated that the chaffinch copies with an accuracy of 85 per cent. In other species only the most common songs are sung from one year to the next. In some cases, these apparent copying errors might occur because the songs heard are distorted by other noises in the bird's environment. Lehtonen (1983), who studied the songs of great tits (*Parus major*) in Finland, believes their songs have become simpler over recent decades because the environment has become more noisy. If this process does occur, we might well contemplate a world in which the songs of birds are degraded to their simplest form. A comparison of the urban members of a species with their conspecifics living in remote, wild environments might be of interest to test this hypothesis, but we would have to consider the potential influence of other factors that could also cause a difference in the songs sung by the two populations.

In fact, we know there is regional variation in the songs sung by birds of the same species. Birds living in one region may sing slightly different songs from those in a nearby region (Slater 1986, 1989). The most common pattern is for the songs to change gradually as their distance apart increases. This spatial variation in the song could be caused by a bird copying different songs of more than one of its neighbours. Thus both time and spatial separation contribute to changes in the songs.

Most emphasis has been placed on the cultural transmission of vocalisations but signalling in other sensory modalities may also be transmitted by learning. It now seems that birds might also be able to learn visual signals as well as vocal signals. This would mean that both visual and vocal signalling could be passed on by cultural transmission.

Vocal learning in nonprimate mammals

Compared with birds, there has been very little research investigating vocal learning in mammals (but see Janik & Slater 1997). In particular, there have been few studies in which mammals have been experimented on by rearing them in isolation, as in birds. This is probably because we have been much more aware of the ethical implications of raising mammals in conditions in which they are deprived of social contact than we have of birds, although this is an artificial distinction because birds are just as dependent on social relations as mammals. The hand-rearing experiments discussed above show this.

To find evidence of vocal learning in mammals in the wild, we can first look to see whether any of them mimic sounds in their environment. Perhaps the best known example of a mammal doing so is that of Hoover, a harbour seal (*Phoca vitulina*) kept in the New England Aquarium in Boston. He learnt to mimic human speech sounds, including, 'Hello there' and 'Come over here'. Sound spectrographs of the seal saying these words and a human saying the same thing have been published by Katherine Ralls and colleagues (1985) of the Smithsonian Institution (see Figure 5.3). The similarities between these spectro-

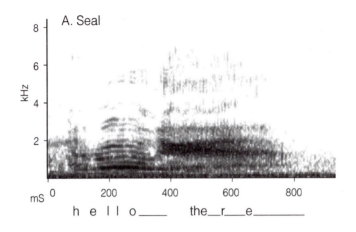

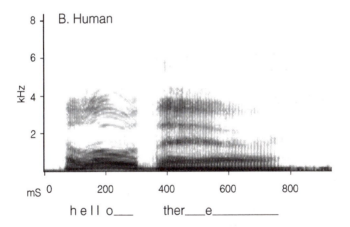

Figure 5.3 Mimicry of human voice by a seal. A. The harbour seal (*Phoca vitulina*), called Hoover, says 'Hello there' with an American accent. B. The same words spoken by a human. (Sound spectrograms produced from an audiotaped recording by Katherine Ralls (via James Scanlon); other examples can be seen in Ralls et al. 1985)

grams are remarkable. Hoover also says, 'Get out of there' and 'Hey', which he strings into sequences with the other sayings and ends with mimicry of human laughter. To the naked ear Hoover sounds like a human with an unnerving slur in the voice and a Boston accent. Another male seal in the same aquarium learnt to say 'Hello', showing that Hoover was not a unique case. Seals can learn human speech sounds when they are in circumstances that favour this type of learning. Hoover was reared without contact with his own species in early life.

It seems that vocal learning may not be uncommon in seals living in their natural environment. There is considerable variation in the vocalisations of members of the same species of seal living in different localities. Although there might be other reasons for spatial variations in vocalisations, these differences indicate that seals might learn their natural calls. It is possible that adult males mimic the calls of males in neighbouring territories, as occurs in songbirds.

There are several species of seals for which geographical variation in vocalisations has been reported but perhaps the best example is that of Weddell seals (*Leptonychotes weddelli*). Separate colonies of Weddell seals living in different fjords in the Vestfold Hills of Antarctica, only 20 kilometres apart, were found to share only five out of a total of 44 different vocalisations (this study was by M.G. Morrice and colleagues, 1994). Even the shared calls were not quite identical. A much earlier study of elephant seals (*Mirounga angustirostris*) inhabiting islands off the west coast of North America, carried out by Burney Le Boeuf and Richard Petersen (1969), found that threat vocalisations made by males vary from one island's population to the next and that these local dialects persisted from generation to generation. This occurred despite the fact that there was some movement of males between islands; the researchers suggested that young males that move to a new island copy the threat calls of the established male population on that island.

Whales kept in captivity have been found to imitate human speech, as first reported by John Lilly (1965). Bottlenose dolphins (*Tursiops truncatis*) mimic their species-specific whistles and they will also learn to mimic whistles that are used in training them to perform tricks. It appears that the dolphins' own whistles can be modified by experience. Diana Reiss and Brenda McCowan (1993) of Marine World Foundation in the United States found that bottlenose dolphins would mimic computer-generated whistles and that they also learnt to produce certain whistles in association with certain interactive behaviours, such as playing with rings or balls. There is no question that the behaviour of dolphins is highly plastic and creative and that this applies to their communication behaviour as well (see also Chapter Four). As far as we know, whales and seals are the most versatile vocal learners of all mammals.

Vocal learning in primates

The other mammalian species in which vocal learning has been investigated to some degree are the primates. We have discussed the remarkable abilities of the great apes to learn sign and symbolic forms of communication by which they can converse with humans. This is ample evidence that they can learn complicated forms of communication. But do they learn their own vocalisations? Unfortunately, there have been surprisingly few studies of the learning of the species-typical calls of any of the apes. Mitani (1994) and colleagues have reported differences in the 'pant hoot' (a loud call) vocalisations of chimpanzees in two different localities in Africa and they have some suggestive evidence that male chimpanzees calling at the same time match their pant-hoot sounds. This indicates that chimpanzee vocalisations can be shaped by learning but more detailed investigations are needed. We summarise what is known of vocalisations made by orang-utans in our book *Orang-utans in Borneo* but these data are patchy and no reliable developmental work has been done.

A study of contact calls in pygmy marmosets (*Cebuella pygmaea*) by Margaret Elowson and Charles Snowdon (1994), of the University of Wisconsin, found that these monkeys modify their trill calls when their social environment is changed so that they can hear the calls of previously unfamiliar members of their own species. They modified both the frequency band width and the peak frequency of their trill calls, and these changes occurred in monkeys of all ages from infants to adults. Thus the trill call, at least, of the pygmy marmoset is plastic, able to change, even in adults. Learning influences the call. Note the similarity to birdsong. The ability to change vocalisations when the social environment changes may be essential to social cohesion in avian and mammalian species.

There is an important study by Robert Seyfarth and Dorothy Cheney (1986) on vervet monkeys (*Cercopithecus aethiops*). They managed to record eagle alarm calls made by 24 infants, 53 juveniles and 55 adults (see Chapters One and Two) in the wild. They also noted the aerial species to which the eagle call was applied. Infants used the call to refer to birds flying overhead but they did not call to all species of eagle and they often called when they caught sight of non-raptor, innocuous species, such as a bee-eater. Compared with the infants, juveniles showed a much greater awareness of different species of eagles although non-raptor and innocuous species, such as a stork, still incorrectly evoked their alarm calls. Adults, by contrast, gave the eagle alarm calls to refer to six different species of eagles, including the goshawk and the owl, and the only non-raptor that evoked their alarm calls was the vulture. However, the call for the vulture was observed to occur in fewer than five cases. The results show that infants use the eagle alarm call rather non-specifically to refer to a wide range of aerial predators, whereas adults have learnt to use the call specifically to refer to raptors. It took nearly two years to collect these data. They show very well that learning the meaning of a call must take place from infancy to adulthood and that the monkeys might have particular images in mind when they produce this alarm call.

Marc Hauser (1988) has discovered that infant vervet monkeys also learn to recognise the alarm calls given by starlings. In Chapter Two we discussed the vervet monkeys' attention to the alarm calls made by starlings that live in the same locality. The adult monkeys are able to exploit this to detect the presence of a predator in the air or on the ground. Given the interspecies nature of this form of signalling, it is not surprising that the vervet monkeys have to learn the meaning of the starlings' calls. Hauser's research was conducted by playing back tape recordings of not only the starlings' ground-predator alarm calls but also their songs. Infants of less than three months of age were able to distinguish between the starlings' alarm calls and their song but they did not interpret the alarm calls as indicating danger. They simply looked at the loudspeaker when it was broadcasting a starling's alarm call but not when it was broadcasting the bird's song. By the time they were three to four months old they had learnt the meaning of the starlings' ground-predator alarm call—they responded to it by scampering up the nearest tree. Moreover, infants that had been exposed to more examples of the starlings' alarm call learnt sooner than those exposed less often. These results need confirmation with more subjects but they demonstrate interspecies learning of vocalisations. This is a very special case of learning.

Learning seems to occur for at least another call made by vervet monkeys. Marc Hauser (1989) studied the age-related changes in the '*wrr*' call that they make when they encounter another troop of vervet monkeys. He found that infants of less than three months old produce a *wrr*-like call when they are distressed by being lost and it is even more like the *wrr* call of adults than that of older infants. Although infants of 10–18 months old produce *wrr* calls during encounters with other groups of monkeys, their calls are not acoustically identical to those of adults. In summary, very young infants (up to three months of age) make *wrr* calls when they are lost and at other times when they seek contact; then there is a period from three to ten months of age when no *wrr* calls are made, followed by *wrr* calls that are not the same as the adults' from ten months to three or four years of age; finally, the adult *wrr* is made after four years of age. This time-course for development of the calls was speeded up in infants belonging to groups that experienced more encounters with other groups of monkeys, which suggests that learning plays a role in the development of the adult call used in a specific context. However, maturation of the vocal apparatus may also contribute to the development that occurs. These transitions in the call which occur with age and/or experience are most interesting and deserve further study. Hauser noted that the period when *wrrs* were not produced (three to ten months old) is also the period when other types of vocalisations are being acquired and this might distract the young monkey from making the *wrr* call (Figure 5.4). When it begins to make the call again the structure of the call might have been degraded and that may be why it has to be learnt again. Similar transitions have been reported to occur in the development of language in human children.

Hauser (1994) has also shown, in a study of rhesus monkeys (*Macaca mulatta*), that the characteristic dominant role of the left hemisphere in processing the species-specific vocalisations is not present in infants. It develops with increasing age. Hauser determined which hemisphere was dominant by scoring which ear the monkeys used to listen to a loudspeaker playing back their calls. Adults favoured the right ear and this means that most of the processing is occurring in the left hemisphere because the auditory input goes mostly to the hemisphere on the opposite side to the ear. Infants showed no preference for one ear over the other. These results do not tell us whether this developmental change in the processing of the vocalisations is influenced by experience, learning or simply maturation, but it is possible that all these processes are involved. We know that experience influences the development of brain asymmetry in birds and learning can affect it, too, as the research of Lesley Rogers (1997) has shown.

Some studies on primates have found less evidence of vocal learning. The calls of the squirrel monkey (*Saimiri sciureus*) have been studied in some detail. Research carried

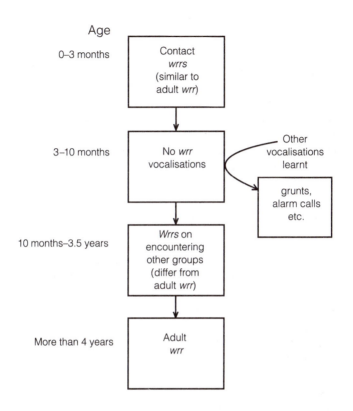

Figure 5.4 Developmental changes in *wrr* calls of vervet monkeys. Adults produce the *wrr* call, a trilled call, during aggressive encounters between neighbouring groups. Babies make a similar call when they become separated from their mothers. Note the period when no *wrr* calls are made, a stage when other calls are being learnt. (After Hauser, M.D. 1989)

out in the early 1980s by Lieblich and colleagues (1980) and by Newman and Symmes (1982) showed that there was little age-dependent change in the calls of squirrel monkeys, and also that the calls were not greatly affected by rearing the monkeys in social isolation from other members of their species. This suggested that the calls of this species were strongly determined by inheritance (i.e. by the genes). However, more recent studies have indicated that this conclusion was incorrect. Maxine Biben and Deborah Bern-hards (1995), of the National Institutes of Health in Maryland, in the United States, have found that the *chuck* calls of young females are more similar to those of members of their own social group than to members of other groups, which suggests that learning is involved. Also there are marked differences in the types of calls that the monkeys make at different ages. Although this does not prove that learning occurs, it does show that there is flexibility in their vocalisations. There appears to be learning of the specificity of when and where these calls should be used.

Overall, it can be said that the present state of knowledge shows that marmosets, tamarins, squirrel monkeys and many other primate species change their vocalisations with devel-opment, as John Newman (1995) of the National Institutes of Health in Maryland has summarised. In addition, we would like to return to a point that we made in Chapter Four: almost all the primate calls that have been studied are the more obvious calls, used for alarm, distress or group contact; the more intimate and softer social calls have been ignored. It would be of much interest to compare the development of these calls with that of the more obvious calls.

Some conclusions on learning to communicate

From extensive research on song learning in birds, we can conclude that learning has a major role during a sensitive period in early life. In some species, no new songs are learnt in adulthood. In other species, such as the canary, adult song remains plastic although seasonal changes in hormone levels determine when singing will occur.

It is simply too early to reach any firm conclusions about the learning of vocal communication in primates, or other mammals, but developmental changes do occur and at least some of these are known to be affected by experience and learning. There are some similarities between species of primates in the way the structure of their vocalisations changes with age. In addition, primates share with birds and humans the stage of vocal development referred to as babbling. Infant primates are very vocal compared with adults, and songbirds perform their highly varied subsong in a manner akin to the babbling of human babies. This would appear to be a stage when the young animal is practising the structure of the vocalisations.

Not only must the structure of calls and song be learnt but so too must the meaning of each call. The studies of Hauser were a step forward because they took into account the meaning of the call and did not just document the changes in the structure of the vocalisations with increasing age. There is enormous scope for more work along these lines.

It should also be noted that there is some evidence that different groups of monkeys belonging to the same species have different dialects (e.g. as Steven Green (1975) has shown to occur in Japanese macaques living in three different locations) and this too may indicate that learning of vocalisation occurs, as we explain for birdsong. With the vervet monkeys, where it is known that the meaning of calls is learnt, it would now be interesting to know whether this type of learning might form a cultural tradition. In fact, we wonder whether the vervet monkeys of Barbados, taken there from Africa many years ago, have retained the same use of alarm calls and use them with the same specificity to refer to predators as do the vervet monkeys in Africa. Even if one generation teaches the calls to the next, the meaning may have changed to some extent with the presence of different predators in the new environment. Some information from the chimpanzees that have learnt sign language shows that signs may be passed on from one generation to the next. Roger Fouts and colleagues (1989) observed Washoe actively teaching her son, Loulis, how to sign: she was observed to mould his hands into the correct sign. This indicates that, in chimpanzees, the mechanisms for an active cultural tradition are in place.

Although most of the research on learning to communicate has focused on vocalisations, it should be remembered that primates, as well as other mammals, also communicate by scent-marking, visual displays and various forms of tactile communication (see Chapters Three and Four). It would be important to investigate whether learning occurs in these other forms of communication. Is there, for example, a stage in development when visual displays are plastic, as occurs for song? It is not unreasonable to suggest that animals might show 'babbling' in visual displays, as they do for vocalisations. In fact, Laura Petitto and Paula Marentette (1991) of McGill University have shown that babbling in humans is not confined to vocal production: deaf children exposed to sign language from birth display manual babbling in which they run through the various hand positions used in signing, just as hearing children do in vocal babbling. Thus, an early phase of development when practice occurs may be related to communication but is not necessarily confined to vocal communication. And, since vocal babbling is not unique to humans, other forms of babbling may be found in animals too. As far as birds are concerned, we know much more about their vocal learning than we do of any other group of animals, but we know virtually nothing of how they develop their visual displays, in all their complexity and variety.

CHAPTER SIX

THE EVOLUTION OF COMMUNICATION

In this chapter, we consider the contribution that the genes make to communication in animals. We examine the aspects of signalling and receiving that may be passed from generation to generation of the species by a program encoded in the genes, as opposed to by learning. As we saw in Chapter Five, many important aspects of signalling are learnt by each animal during the course of its life, particularly during its early life. However, learning is not the only factor involved. All the behaviours that are used in communication depend on the interaction between genetic factors and learning. Some researchers who write about signalling in animals give the impression that signals are largely under the control of genes and that genetic evolution has been the main process by which signalling has changed over time and from species to species. While we do not deny that genetic evolution has a role, signals can be learnt and passed on from generation to generation, as we saw in the discussion of the cultural transmission of song in Chapter Five.

Although it is known that, in insects, some forms of simple behaviour are programmed by the genes, this should not be extrapolated to the more complex behaviours that are used by higher animals for communication. Almost all the forms of communication discussed in this book depend to various degrees on learning. However this does not mean that they are entirely divorced from all genetic contributions.

It is difficult, if not impossible, to look at the behaviour of the signaller or the receiver and say how much of that behaviour is determined by the genes and how much depends on learning because both influences interact so completely and there is so much variation from one animal to another. On this point we differ from many ethologists and evolutionary biologists who see genes as having a tangible and direct causal influence on all signalling behaviour and are often prepared to ignore questions about learning and development of that behaviour.

In Chapters Four and Five, we discussed the experiments performed with songbirds reared in isolation so that they could not hear other members of their own species singing. These birds sing abnormal songs but retain a template of the song. At first this result was interpreted to mean that the genes determined the template and then learning elaborated upon that to give the full song. In other words, each bird was said to inherit a foundation for its song, on which it builds by the process of learning that occurs when the young bird hears other birds singing. However, the experiments in which birds were deafened in early life (see Chapter Five for our view on the ethics of this procedure) showed that even the template of the song is no longer present if the bird cannot hear itself sing. We have discussed the methodological problems with this sort of sensory deprivation experiment (in Chapter Five, especially, but also in other chapters) but the result does indicate that the earlier notion that genes alone determine the template for song may be incorrect, unless the effect of hearing no sound led to degradation of an existing template.

Nevertheless, genes do specify some broad aspects of the sensory systems that a particular species will have available to perceive signals (e.g. a sensory system for seeing certain wavelengths of light; ultrasound detection; the ability to detect currents of electricity). This determines the nature of the signals that will be most effective for the species. Genes may also specify aspects of the structures that will be used to produce signals (e.g. the colours and sizes of feathers or the construction of the syrinx). In these cases, we may look on the genetic factors as constraints that influence the development of the structures and behaviours used for signalling, or as constraints on the development of sensory organs and the other processes that are used to detect, discriminate and interpret the meaning of the signal. The number of such genetic constraints on the development of the behaviour of a species varies from species to species and from one form of signal display to another but, in every case, they are broad constraints. They do not occur at a level that will determine the exact details of the behaviour patterns used in communication.

Often, learning is not merely an elaboration, or fine-tuning, of a basic template that has been specified by the genes. In many cases, experience can completely change the original genetic prescription so that it is no longer recognisable. The sensory capabilities of an animal depend on experience, as shown so clearly in kittens that were given an abnormal visual experience just after they opened their eyes. Colin Blakemore, of Cambridge University, discovered that a kitten that has been allowed to see only vertical black and white stripes for a short period after it first opens its eyes is unable to see horizontal stripes for the rest of its life (Blakemore & Cooper 1970). The early experience so modifies the way the kitten processes visual information that, from then on, it does not respond to an object that is waved back and forth horizontally, whereas it runs to play with one that is moved up and down vertically. The opposite is true of a kitten exposed to horizontal stripes instead of vertical ones.

At first, this might seem as if the genes make absolutely no contribution to the kitten's ability to see. However, a kitten that is kept in the dark over the same period of time as the others were exposed to the stripes is able to see both vertical and horizontal stripes, and indeed stripes at any angle. Therefore, the ability of the kitten to be able to see stripes at any angle when it first opens its eyes appears to be determined genetically, unless another form of environmental stimulation acting before the eyes open has some influence also. Visual experience immediately after the eyes open has a critical effect in changing the way the visual system is wired up, and it determines what the kitten will be able to see from that time on (i.e. what signals it will see). In the normal environment, a kitten would see lines at all angles and thus the early visual experience would reinforce the genetic plan. Only by putting the kitten in an abnormal visual environment can the importance of learning be shown.

We use this example of early experience in the kitten to illustrate the interaction of genes and early experience and, in this case, the overriding role of experience during a sensitive period of life. A similar effect of early experience has been shown by one of the authors (Rogers 1995, 1996) to affect the development of the nerve connections that are used to process visual inputs in the chicken. Light exposure of the chick embryo just before hatching stimulates the development of nerve cells that connect the chick's midbrain to its forebrain. In fact, because the embryo is oriented in the egg so that its head is turned with the left side against its body, only the right eye is stimulated by the light; it is the connections to this eye only that are stimulated to grow and so an asymmetry develops. If chicks are hatched from eggs that have been incubated in the dark, no such asymmetry develops and there are fewer connections from both eyes. The visual behaviour of the chick is also altered in ways that would be expected from the differences in the visual connections between chicks that have had exposure to light and those that have not. Chicks exposed to light before hatching can find grains of food scattered on a background of small pebbles when they are tested with a patch over the left eye but not when the patch is over the right eye. Chicks hatched from eggs incubated in the dark do not show this asymmetry. This is another example of experience in early life altering the way that subsequent information is perceived and processed by the brain.

Just like the effect of this early visual experience, what an animal learns in early life can also radically modify its subsequent behaviour. The examples of song learning given in Chapter Five illustrated this point. There are critical ages at which animals must be exposed to certain stimuli or at which they must learn certain things and, if this does not happen, they will not develop in a way that is typical for the species. This applies to the behaviours used in communication as much as to any other behaviour. Perhaps the most important thing to say here is that social behaviour and social learning in early life has many and various effects on the communication abilities and patterns that an animal develops.

It is, of course, essential for communication between members of the same species that all individuals share the same communication system, although there may be regional variations and also seasonal and age variations. Each individual's use of the common communication system can be established by social learning. It does not have to be programmed by the genes, although sometimes it is assumed that the commonality of a particular signalling system implies that it is entirely genetically determined. Such a view may have its roots in seeing animals as mechanistic and behaviour as fixed action patterns. It denies the fact that behaviour patterns can be learnt consistently and well, with little variation between individuals or from one generation to the next.

We find it necessary to stress the role of learning because, all too frequently, ethologists who are interested in the evolution of displays and other forms of communication tend to give it only passing recognition and then proceed to discuss evolution without any further mention of learning. We ask the reader to keep this in mind as we discuss the commonality of communication systems within and between species. When we speak of evolution, we are referring to the process of genetic selection. We do not deny that this process occurs but signals may also be passed from generation to generation by learning and these two processes are not separate. Unless the genetic and experiential contributions to a particular behaviour pattern have been studied in detail, we will not follow the all-too-common practice of assuming that genes have the overriding role in determining the behaviour pattern. We note that evolutionary biologists do not think that the entirety of the signalling behaviour is determined by the genes but, in our view, they often place far too much emphasis on the genetic determinants at the expense of experience and learning. Also, their genetic explanations for the complex behaviour that animals use to communicate tend to trivialise the processes of development.

How do communication patterns come about?

Many animal displays look so bizarre to us that we wonder how they came about. By the same token, many human displays probably look equally bizarre to animals. Most of the various forms of signalling that are used by different species of animals have not arisen afresh in each separate species. As one species evolves into another, particular forms of signalling may be passed on at the same time, determined by both genes and learning or experience. As we explained in Chapters Three and Four, some signals have significance across many species. However, as they are passed from generation to generation by whatever means, signals may go through changes that make them more elaborate or simply different. If we examine closely related species, we can often see slight variations in a particular display and we can piece together a plan for the spread of the display across species, just as for the formation of song dialects (see Chapters Three and Five). Some very elaborate displays may have begun as simpler versions of the same behavioural patterns, as we discuss below.

But how might signals or displays have come about in the first place? Some displays appear to have developed from movements when the animal is getting ready to perform a particular behaviour. These are known as 'intention movements'. Other signals may have come about by elaborating particular parts of a display. Sometimes the part of a display that is elaborated upon appears to be irrelevant to the situation in which it occurs. For this reason, it has been called a 'displacement' activity (although it is now debated whether the activity is really displaced or outside of context and that is why we will continue to use the term 'displacement' within quote marks). For example, two cocks threatening to fight may sometimes break off their aggressive display directed at each other and peck at the ground with the beak closed. This so-called 'titbitting' behaviour has been considered to be a 'displacement' activity because it is not obviously relevant to the display of aggression. The conclusion that titbitting is irrelevant in this context might have been made only because we are unable to interpret the animal's behaviour accurately enough to know what it really means. It could be relevant and we simply cannot see that this is so, as Marian Dawkins, of Oxford University, said in her book published in 1986.

Another kind of behaviour that has been referred to as 'displacement' behaviour in many contexts is grooming or preening. A cat that is anxious to be fed but cannot persuade its owner to open the refrigerator may suddenly stop meowing and rubbing on its owner's legs and switch to licking itself, or a bird that is in conflict about whether it should eat a prey that it has not seen before may switch its attention away from the prey and preen itself briefly. In both these examples, the act of grooming or preening appears to be irrelevant to the main theme of the behaviour pattern in which it occurs. As we may see it as irrelevant behaviour only through our ignorance of its function or purpose, it may be better to refer to it as 'redirected' behaviour rather than 'displacement' behaviour. The performance of such redirected behaviour may be observed and interpreted by another animal, in which case it serves as a signal.

Both intention movements and those behaviours that have previously been called 'displacement' behaviours may be modified to signal to other animals. In addition, the physical and behavioural adjustments that animals make to maintain their physiological function (e.g. to maintain body temperature within the correct range) may be used to signal.

We will discuss each of these in more detail. The point to stress here is that many elaborate displays appear to have evolved from simple behaviours that animals perform in their everyday life. These simple behaviours may also signal in subtle ways but they become signals that are more obvious to the human observer when they have been exaggerated and so have become ritualised. We discuss mostly the more exaggerated signals in this chapter, although we recognise that the less obvious signals may be just as important.

Intention movements

First we must distinguish between intention movements, which we are discussing in this chapter, and intentional signalling, discussed in Chapter Two. In Chapter Two we were concerned with the issue of whether animals merely emit information that signals their emotional state or deliver planned communication in which signals are performed after making decisions about the context and other factors important at the time. In this case, we used the term 'intentional' to refer to the state of mind of the signaller, or at least to the cognitive processes involved in signalling. In this chapter, we use the term 'intention movements', as used by ethologists, to refer to those behaviours performed in preparation for an activity. Such behaviours signal what the animal is about to do next but they do not, in themselves, tell us anything about whether the animal thinks about performing them as opposed to performing them uncontrollably and without any form of thought. It is possible that the more ritualised these behaviours become— and so the more obvious they are as signals—the more likely they will be performed with at least some of the intentionality we referred to in Chapter Two, but there has been virtually no research on this topic.

The first example of an intention movement that we consider is the preparation for flight in birds. Before they take off into flight, many birds crouch, raise the tail and withdraw the head (Figure 6.1a and 6.1b) and then stretch

Figure 6.1 Flight intention postures and displays. A and B. Flight intention movements. Crouching and raising the tail (A) is followed by lowering the tail and stretching the head and neck in the intended direction of flight (B), and this may be repeated several times before the bird takes off. C and D. Displays of the green heron (*Butorides virescens*), which incorporate aspects of flight intention movements. C. The forward threat display adopted in territorial defence. D. The stretch display performed as a prelude to mating. E. The head and tail up posture of the kookaburra (*Dacelo gigas*) when it is making its territorial laughing call. (After McFarland 1985 and Smith 1977)

the body in the direction of the intended flight. A bird may adopt this posture several times before it takes off and thereby it signals to other members of the flock that it is about to fly. It has been observed that a pigeon does not usually disturb the other members of its flock if it performs flight intention movements before taking off but, if it flies off suddenly without these intention movements, the whole of the flock is likely to take to the air.

Richard Andrew (1956), of Sussex University, has studied in detail the flight intention movements of certain species and the involvement of head bobbing and tail flicking in many social displays. These aspects of the flight intention movements have been incorporated into signalling patterns (displays). In some cases the meaning of the signal appears to be quite removed from the original intention movement. For example, the American green heron signals pair formation and courtship by adopting a posture in which the head is withdrawn, the beak held in the air and the feathers on the head sleeked down (Figure 6.1d). This appears to be a modified flight intention movement and it contrasts with the species' aggressive display in which the beak is pointed forward, the feathers are ruffled and the tail is vibrated (Figure 6.1c). The aggressive display also has elements of flight intention movements but it includes aiming of the bird's weapon (the beak) at its opponent. The kookaburra (*Dacelo gigas*) also displays a posture of modified flight intention when it makes its territorial call, which sounds like laughing (Figure 6.1e).

Similarly, a seagull about to attack stretches its neck out horizontally and directs its beak at its opponent, as Niko Tinbergen (1960, 1965), of Oxford University, so clearly described for herring gulls. Tinbergen also described the upright threat posture of the herring gull, in which the neck is stretched upwards and the head pointed downwards (Figure 6.2a). Having adopted this posture, the gull struts towards its opponent. The positioning of the head and neck is exactly the posture that a gull adopts in circumstances in which it actually pecks its opponent. When used as a threat display, but without actually pecking, it is a strong signal that the bird is about to attack. In this case, the intention movement of pecking has been used as a signal to display aggression.

Displaying of weapons is also characteristic of aggressive or threat displays in mammals. When a dog is about to attack, for example, it bares its teeth in preparation for biting. As we saw in Chapter Four, bared teeth has become a display that signals aggression in many mammals. However, we need to add that the bared-teeth display is accompanied by changes in the eyes, ears and body posture of the dog. Only by taking all these features into account can we accurately interpret the meaning of the bared-teeth display (see Andrew 1965). A dog with its teeth bared, eyes open wide, ears erect (Figure 6.2b) and tail up in a confident posture is threatening but one with teeth bared, eyes almost closed, ears flattened (Figure 6.2c) and tail down between its legs is afraid and will flee unless it is cornered, when it will attack. The latter display indicates that the dog is feeling a mixture of aggression and fear.

There are many other examples in which the showing of weapons signals that the animal is about to attack. A bull (Figure 6.2d) or a deer (Figure 6.2e) about to attack lowers his head and orients his horns at the object of his aggression. These are all postures adopted in preparation for an actual attack but, in the display itself, they do not actually lead to an attack on the opponent. Instead they are examples of intention movements being used to signal the possibility of aggression. Most such displays of aggression end with one animal backing off, thereby avoiding serious injury.

'Displacement' behaviours

We gave the example of titbitting in cocks as 'displacement' behaviour, on the grounds that, when it interrupts aggressive displaying, it appears to be unrelated to the main purpose

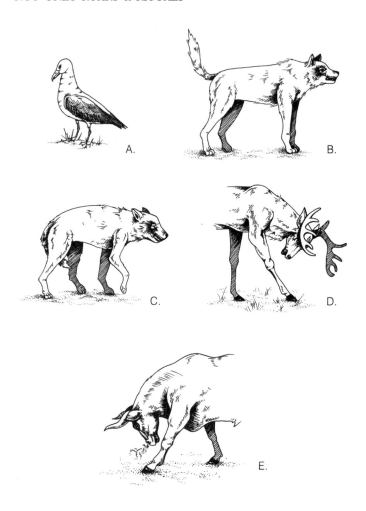

Figure 6.2 Threat postures. A. A herring gull adopting an upright threat posture. B. Dog with teeth bared, eyes opened wide, ears forward and tail up in confident threat posture. C. Dog with teeth bared, eyes almost closed, ears flattened and tail lowered in a defensive threat posture, indicating a high level of fear. D. A deer threatening to attack by displaying its weapons. E. A bull threatening in a similar way.

of the display. It involves pecking at small objects on the ground without picking them up and, therefore, does not appear to be related to the goal of feeding either. It may, however, have a function in relieving tension briefly and thus reducing the chance of an actual attack occurring. Cocks often threaten each other at the borders of their territories and here each animal is in a conflict between approaching (and being attacked) and fleeing. 'Displacement' or redirected (see earlier) activities often occur when an animal feels conflict. Titbitting is one example and, by observing this behaviour, another animal might recognise the position of the border of the territory. In other words, the 'displacement' behaviour might become a signal. Of course, once it has become a signal it can no longer be called a 'displacement' activity because it has a genuine function related to the context in which it occurs. Taken together with our earlier point about the so-called irrelevance of 'displacement' behaviours being merely a matter of our inability to understand them, this consideration makes the term 'displacement' behaviour very problematic. Nevertheless, despite objections to the term, these *apparently* irrelevant behaviours exist and elaboration upon them does appear to explain some forms of signalling.

So-called 'displacement' preening is one of the most often cited cases. When such preening or grooming occurs, it may signal that the animal is in a state of conflict. We mentioned the cat that grooms itself when thwarted from obtaining food. This is a form of approach–withdrawal conflict. The cat decides to lick itself instead of either approaching or withdrawing. Courtship behaviour often involves conflict about whether to approach or withdraw and this might explain why preening or grooming often occurs in courtship displays. In 1941 the Austrian ethologist, Konrad Lorenz, described preening as a feature of courtship displays in ducks (see also Lorenz 1965). Shelducks (*Tadorna tadorna*) turn the head to preen feathers on the back or wings during courtship. This is considered to be a displacement activity. The mallard duck (*Anas platyrhynchos*) does likewise but restricts its preening to brightly coloured feathers on the wing. Preening reveals the feathers that have been specialised as part of the display. In the mallard the preening has become stylised, or ritualised. In the garganey duck (*Anas querquedula*) the ritualisation is even greater; this species rubs its beak on specialised blue feathers on the outside of the wings in a way that mimics preening, although preening does not actually take place. The court-ship display of the mandarin duck (*Aix galericulata*) has the greatest degree of ritualisation of all these species. The mandarin duck does not actually preen but mimics the preening of two specialised secondary feathers which project up from its wings by touching them once only with the beak. The ritualisation of the preening motion, and also the specialised feathers themselves, are an elaboration that has evolved from the simple act of preening. The display is enhanced by the enlargement of the particular feathers that the duck touches with his beak and their rust-red colour which makes them stand out from the other feathers. A crest on the back of the head is also raised, increasing the ritualisation of the behaviour. In other words, the mandarin duck performs an exaggerated and highly specific display.

Differences between species in courtship displays may help to isolate closely related species from one another in situations where they live in overlapping territories. By using different courtship signals, cross-breeding may be prevented. No confusion between species occurs as long as the signals to mate are different for each species. In cases where this occurs, there is an intimate relationship between the evo-lution of a species and its communication signals.

In time, what might have begun as 'displacement' (or redirected) preening during the courtship display has become a more specific signal. This example shows how signals might evolve, although it remains possible that learning has an essential role in establishing the final pattern of the display. Other examples of ritualisation of displace-ment behaviours have been described. Feeding of the female by the male is an aspect of courtship in many species, from gulls to budgerigars. The female begs for food much as the young do. When the male feeds the female during courtship, it is considered to be 'displacement' behaviour because it is not his goal at the time. In some species of birds, as we saw in Chapter Three, the behaviour is ritualised by the giving of gifts in courtship. Like preening during courtship, feeding is part of the signalling process, saying perhaps 'I like you', or 'I am willing to provide food for you and our offspring'. Incidentally, this ritual also occurs in the courtship behaviour of humans.

Autonomic responses used as signals

Some of the behavioural and physical adjustments that animals must perform to maintain their physiological state are also used to signal. These are known as autonomic responses because they are controlled by the autonomic nervous system. In humans, we know that these responses occur automatically, without conscious control. For example, in cases of extreme fear, the hair on our bodies is raised in preparation for cooling, necessary if we need to flee. Other autonomic responses occur also, but here we are interested in this particular one because raising of the hair is also common in other mammals. This fluffing of the hair, termed piloerection, functions as a signal of fear. In marmosets (*Callithrix* sp.) and tamarins (*Saguinus* sp.) fluffing of the tail, due to piloerection, signals fear and indicates that the monkey is more likely to flee than approach.

Richard Andrew (1972) was the first to point out the importance of autonomic responses in displays. He also noted that the raising and lowering of the feathers for autonomic control of body temperature has become a feature of many avian displays. Feather raising is quite difficult to interpret because slight raising (fluffing) of the feathers encloses air around the body and provides insulation for heat loss, whereas further raising causes ruffling of the feathers as their tips no longer touch each other and heat is lost because air is no longer trapped around the body. Ruffling often occurs in aggressive displays, when cooling might be needed, and fluffing often occurs when a bird is quiet and submissive. Laughing gulls, for example, perform an aggressive display in which they lower the head and jerk it rhythmically while making a deep call and ruffling the feathers. Galahs also indicate threat or aggression by ruffling the feathers (Figure 6.3). Sleeking of the feathers is another way to increase heat loss and it appears in the aggressive displays of some species. It also appears commonly in states of high arousal and, as such, it has become incorporated into the camouflage posture of tawny frogmouths when a predator is near (see Figure 3.1).

Urination and defecation are other autonomic responses that occur in a state of high arousal, as evoked by very frightening stimuli. Not surprisingly, therefore, urination and defecation are used by some animals as part of fear or threat displays. Tawny frogmouths will often turn and spray their extremely pungent faeces at a predator approaching from below (more detail on tawny frogmouths in Chapter Three). When bushbabies (galagos, lower primates) mob a predator they frequently urinate on their hands and rub the urine on their bodies, while making warning vocalisations and adopting threatening postures. The autonomic responses have become incorporated into the threat display.

The autonomic nervous system also controls the constriction and dilation of the pupils in the eyes. In Chapter Two, we saw that pupil size changes with emotional state and that it is assessed by observers even though they are not conscious of using this information. This is an aspect of autonomic function that is used involuntarily in communication. We should note, however, that in the past humans have consciously used drugs to dilate the pupils to enhance their attractiveness. Dilated pupils give the face a more seductive appearance and women used to put drops of the antimuscarinic drug, belladonna, into their eyes to dilate the pupils. This was at

Figure 6.3 Feather ruffling in a galah. A. Sleek posture. B. Feathers ruffled in an aggressive or threat posture. Both photographs are of the same galah. Note that in B the body feathers are raised and the feathers on the cheeks are elevated to an almost horizontal position, making the bird appear much larger than it is. (Photographs by G. Kaplan)

the expense of being able to see clearly—the drug also paralyses the muscle by which focus of the lens in the eye is achieved. In this case, signalling must have been seen as more important than receiving signals!

Why do signals become ritualised?

A ritualised signal is one that is exaggerated, stereotyped and often repeated. Quite obviously, a stereotyped signal states its point clearly and ritualisation makes sure that the signal is not easily confused with any other signal. This is advantageous in itself, but there may be another reason why signals become stereotyped. As Desmond Morris suggested in 1957, because ritualised signals are so stylised, they give away less information about the internal state of the sender than signals that are simpler intention movements, 'displacement' behaviours or autonomic responses. The last three types of signal tell us more about the emotional state of the sender or indicate whether the sender is balanced between attacking and fleeing. In a sense, ritualisation involves a loss of detailed information about the sender. However, as Morris suggests, ritualisation may have come about precisely because it conceals this kind of information. Ritualisation may be the signal-sender's way of manipulating the receiver without giving away too much about itself.

If it is the case that the sender is attempting to manipulate the receiver, then the receiver might be advantaged by attempting to ignore the sender. The results of this might be increased ritualisation by the sender, then increased ignoring by the receiver, and so on until the bizarre occurs! This 'arms-race' explanation for ritualisation differs from the hypothesis that ritualisation came about to avoid signal confusion. It is, in fact, a far more beguiling view of animal communication, and one that seems to appeal to more people in a modern, Western world where advertising is used to manipulate us all. Despite this appeal, there is no proof as to which hypothesis is more correct.

We emphasise again that, so far, researchers have been concerned with studying the obvious, ritualised signals that animals perform. More attention to the subtle, quieter and less bizarre signals may change our views on the reasons for, and the evolution of, all these signals. That is something for the future.

Despite the fact that ritualisation may conceal the sender's internal state, few signals, ritualised or not, conceal the physique (strength or weakness, state of health) of the sender. In fact, some signalling may be used precisely to advertise the sender's physical prowess. Stotting is a behaviour performed by Thomson's gazelles (Chapter One). On some occasions, when a predator is approaching, they perform springing jumps into the air (stotting) instead of running away. Although it was first thought that this was a visual signal to warn other gazelles in the herd to flee, Amotz Zahavi (1979) suggests that stotting is, instead, directed at the predator, signalling the gazelle's physical fitness and therefore its ability to escape. Fitzgibbon and Fanshaw (1988) provide some evidence confirming this idea. They found that a predator is more likely to attack a gazelle that stots at a low rate than one that is in better physical condition and can stot at a high rate. The stotting of the gazelles is seen as an 'honest' signal, as Zahavi called it, showing the predator what the gazelle can actually do, rather than being a form of manipulation.

Evolution of features to enhance signalling

We have mentioned the specialised wing feathers that ducks preen during courtship displays. The behaviour pattern of ritualised preening evolved along with the specialised structure of the feathers. The behavioural act of ritualised preening draws attention to these specialised feathers and the feathers, in turn, enhance the behavioural act itself.

The most striking example showing feathers used for the purpose of display is the male peacock's train. The train has evolved to be so large that it is a considerable handicap to the general aspects of survival. Yet this disadvantage is balanced against its effectiveness as a courtship signal. Raising the tail and bowing the head is a feature of courtship displays in other species of the pheasant family (including chickens and pheasants) and fanning of the tail accompanies these acts in other related species. The peacock courtship display is thought to have evolved from these simpler displays by exaggerating the structure by which he signals in terms of both its size and visual attractiveness. The hundreds of eye-spots (ocelli) are attractive to humans as well as peahens. Marion Petrie, Tim Halliday and Carolyn Sanders (1991), at the Open University in the United Kingdom, have shown that peahens choose to mate with peacocks with the largest number of spots on the train. This demonstrates how the apparently oversized, ornate train is likely to have evolved despite the handicap it is for moving around or fleeing from a predator.

There are other features that enhance displays. A coloured beak makes displays with the beak more obvious and contrasting coloured skin, feathers or fur around the eyes enhances any display using the eyes. The colouration around the eyes occurs quite commonly in birds and mammals. The colour of the iris may also enhance displays in which the eyes are featured. The size of the pupil of the eye is more obvious if the iris is a light colour. In fact, a dark-coloured iris might be used to conceal the size of the pupil. It is interesting to note that the only way that humans can distinguish the sex of galahs (*Catacua roseicapella*, an Australian cockatoo) is by the colour of the iris, males having a dark-brown iris and females a pink iris. The sex difference in the colour of the iris would mean that males can detect the size of the female's pupil but females cannot so easily do likewise for the male's pupil. Signalling of emotional state by pupil size (see Chapter Two) might, therefore, in this species, be a female-to-male signal but not vice versa.

Evolution of sensory systems and processing of signals

So far we have discussed the evolution of signals but communication requires not only a signaller but also a receiver; evolutionary changes may occur on the receiver side of the dyad, as well as on the sender side, as outlined by Tim Guilford and Marian Dawkins (1991) of Oxford University. They refer to evolutionary changes in the sensory receptors used for detecting the signal as well as in the processes that are used to discriminate one signal from another and decode or interpret the message that has been transmitted. In addition, they postulate that evolution of memory processes may occur and affect signalling—the receiver often has to remember which animal sent the signal, whether the signal had been sent previously and in what context.

Could genes act to improve the capacity for processing and remembering a signal? As we saw from the example of the kitten exposed to stripes, experience can have profound effects on sensory perception. Experience also has great effects on signal interpretation and the memory processes involved in communication. Recognition of these radical effects of experience and learning leads us to believe that any hypothesis which considers only the evolutionary issues of genetic selection of these abilities is one-sided and too simple. Although genetic selection for some aspects of sensory perception, and even for some aspects of brain processing that might be used for attention, discrimination, decoding and memorising, must certainly occur, it cannot be separated from the effects of experience and learning on the same processes and should not be discussed separately, except in very general terms. We can speak of the evolution of the structure of the eye, for example, and consider how it changed over evolutionary time from one species to the next, but it becomes problematic when we speak of evolutionary changes that might have been involved

173

in the processes of memory, interpretation and attention, since these are so malleable by experience.

Of course, as the brain evolved, its capacity to process information and to store memories increased overall but even a very simple brain can process, detect, decode and remember the signals that are appropriate for the species. A more highly evolved brain can process and remember a greater number and range of signals (i.e. it has increased capacity) but it might not be any better than a simple brain for any single signal. This is another reason why we think that talking about the genetic selection of increased capacity to process and memorise a single type of signal is problematic. Discussions of genetic selection might be better confined to tangible elements of the sensory receptors that are used to detect the signal and perform some of the initial aspects of discriminating the signal from the background. Here, single genes can influence a single factor, such as the presence of a particular visual pigment (so affecting colour vision, as we discuss next). In such cases, it is not so difficult to make a link between genes and function. The more complex processes of decoding the signal and remembering that go on at higher levels of cognition in the brain are far from dependent on a single gene, and are so influenced by learning and experience, that they would be better left out of discussions of genetic selection because it is an oversimplification to attempt to say they are determined by genes in any unitary way.

As an example of evolutionary contribution to the receiving of signals, let us consider specialisations of the eye in vertebrates. We do this by taking some illustrative examples. The eye of the frog is specialised to detect certain stimuli: there are cells in the retina that respond specifically to small spots, about the size of an insect, as long as these spots are, or have been, moving. The retinal cells are called 'bug detectors'. They have an obvious role in the feeding behaviour of frogs but they might also be important in signalling behaviour. It is as if the eye of the frog is a filter that allows the frog to attend to certain stimuli in preference to others. The same filter could be used for prey catching and signalling. Hence, visual signals used by frogs would be attended to more actively if they involved the movement of small stimuli. In fact, two species of frog (*Staurois parvus* of Brunei and *Taudactylus eugellenis* of Australia) have been observed to signal during courtship by holding up an opened front paw, or a hind limb, and waving it. Each of the frog's digits with their rounded ends would make a spot-like image on the receiver's retina and the waving would provide movement. This would be an ideal visual stimulus for the bug detectors in the retina. The visual signal has been matched to the filtered visual capabilities of the frog. We should mention that auditory signals are a specialisation of frogs and toads and these too have been matched to the filtered auditory perception of the species. The hearing of a particular species of frog or toad is optimal exactly within the narrow range of frequencies (pitches) that they use for vocal signalling.

The retina of a bird's eye contains oil droplets of different colours that are located next to the cells that respond to stimulation by light (the photoreceptors). The oil droplets act as a kind of filter allowing the bird to attend more to some coloured stimuli than to others. Exactly which colour will be more attractive depends on the colour of the oil droplets a species has and also the visual pigments present in the photoreceptors (see later). Chicks (*Gallus gallus*) have pink oil droplets and they prefer to peck at red and yellow food grains. In addition to the filter in the retina, other processes in the brain might be involved in determining the red and yellow preference but, nevertheless, the oil droplets are thought to play a role. The preference for pecking at small red and yellow objects might have evolved because most of the grains that chickens eat in the wild are red to yellow in colour. Once this colour preference had evolved, it could have been applied to signalling behaviour. Later in life, chickens develop red combs that signal their sex, state of health and hormonal status. A preference for 'seeing red' would enhance the signalling capacity of the comb. Thus the filtering of sensory perception, which might have applied first to feeding, might be exploited for sexual and aggressive displays in later life.

To give further examples of the relationship between the make-up of cells in the retina of the eye and the visual abilities used in signalling and other behaviours, we will consider colour vision in more detail. An animal's ability to see colour depends on the presence of colour pigments in receptor cells of the retina, and the presence of these is determined by the genes. Humans have three such pigments (red, green and blue) and that allows us to see the wavelengths of light spanning from red to violet. Because of these three pigments we are said to have trichromatic vision. Many other species of mammals have trichromatic vision also but there are some that have only two colour pigments and they are called dichromates. In fact, the marmoset (*Callithrix jacchus*), the tamarin (*Saguinus fuscicollis*) and the squirrel monkey (*Saimiri sciureus*), all South American monkeys (called platyrrhine monkeys), are special cases in which all the males are dichromates together with some of the females, while the rest of the females are trichromates. This means that the trichromatic females can see a greater range of colours than either the males or the dichromatic females, giving them a better chance of success in finding ripe fruit in the dappled and changing light of the rainforest (see Chapter One for light conditions in the forest). The mechanism for the sex difference is that the genes determining the pigments are carried on the X chromosome (chromosomes being strings of genes located in the nucleus of each cell in the body). The X chromosome also determines an individual's sex.

If trichromatic colour vision is an advantage in finding fruit, why has it not conferred such a selective advantage on the trichromates that they have completely replaced the dichromates? Why have the dichromates not disappeared from existing populations of platyrrhine monkeys? It is possible that this evolutionary process is still in progress and that eventually the dichromates will be replaced by trichromates, but it is perhaps more likely that being a dichromate provides an individual with some other advantage that a trichromate lacks. Dichromates may be able to penetrate certain forms of camouflage and so detect prey that trichromates cannot. This ability might be useful for finding foods other than ripe fruits, such as insects and nuts, which these monkeys also eat. Thus, a mixed population of dichromates and trichromates would have a superior combined searching strategy than a single population of trichromates and, since these monkeys alert each other to the food they find, the combined knowledge would be shared.

The dichromatic and trichromatic forms of colour vision might also have different advantages in detecting different kinds of signalling. Marmosets, for example, use their tails as well as their faces in visual signalling. Their long tails have dark and light stripes that would be seen easily against a dappled background by dichromates, whereas the face has yellowish skin which changes hue, as we have seen, in different states of arousal or sexual condition. This colour change would be seen more clearly by trichromates. Thus groups of marmosets may consist of two types of individuals who pay different amounts of attention to different signals. This idea has yet to be tested.

Colour vision is present in a large number of species. Most species of birds can see colour better than we can and they make full use of their colour vision in displays using coloured feathers of rich variety. Many avian species have as many as four visual pigments in the retina: they are tetrachromates. It is known that several species of birds (e.g. pigeons, starlings and zebra finches) can see ultraviolet light, meaning that they can see shorter wavelengths of light than humans can. Indeed, it is likely that perception of ultraviolet is widespread in birds, and Andrew Bennett (1997) and colleagues, of the University of Bristol, have shown recently that the ultraviolet colours in the plumage of starlings and zebra finches are used in mating displays.

The only reptiles that we know to have been tested for colour vision are two species of turtle and they have excellent colour vision. It is more than likely that other reptiles can see colour also: we have already remarked on the use of colour changes in displays by such reptiles as chameleon lizards. In fact, colour vision evolved much earlier than reptiles, as a visit to a tropical coral reef makes eminently clear: here the fish are brightly coloured and they use these colours in their displays. Bees also have colour vision. Examination of those species that have colour vision and those that do not has led researchers to conclude that colour vision evolved separately several times over in different branches of evolution (Neumeyer 1990). These separate appearances testify to the selective advantage that colour vision confers on a species, although only in environments in which colour can be discriminated.

In Chapter One we saw that many rainforest birds are brightly coloured and that they use these colours to signal. The scarlet macaw (*Ara macao*) of the South American rainforest and the various birds of paradise that inhabit the rainforests of New Guinea stand out perhaps, with their spectacular plumage, above all other birds. In contrast with the wide variety of colours of the forest-dwelling birds, seabirds are more uniform, mainly black or brown and white. This is because the sea is a much more uniform environment and it is also very 'glary'. Colour is not easily distinguished against the glare of the sea or sky and the ability to see colour would not be a high priority in this environment. Seabirds may, however, find colour a useful means of signalling at close range and where the amount of reflection is low. This is exemplified by the yellow beak of the herring gull with its bright red spot, at which the gull chick pecks when the adult returns to the nest with a crop full of fish. The peck by the chick triggers the adult to regurgitate the fish and feed the chick.

Colour vision is not useful to nocturnal species so it was lost along the evolutionary path to humans. The earliest primates, the prosimians, are nocturnal and they have either very limited colour vision or are completely colour-blind, even though they evolved from species that, it appears, were able to see colour. The primates that evolved later in evolutionary time may have 'rediscovered' the colour vision that their ancestors had lost and they did so when they became diurnal (active during the day) and could benefit from having colour vision (Mollon 1990; Neumeyer 1990). Alternatively, it could be argued that the extinct ancestor of both the prosimians and the higher primates was not, in fact, colour-blind and the loss of colour vision in present-day prosimians is a more recent development.

Since the colour vision of the diurnal primates of the Old World (Africa and Asia as opposed to South America) is trichromatic, it is thought to have evolved together with feeding on coloured fruits. Once it had evolved, colour vision could be used for displays in primates. The displays of many diurnal primates depend on colours, whereas those of the nocturnal ones do not. The prosimians are mostly dull-coloured or have black and white stripes, as does *Lemur catta* on its tail. Among the later-evolving, diurnal species, the mandrill (*Mandrillus sphinx*) is the most striking exploiter of colour, with a red and white striped snout and pink to blue skin on and around the genital area. Other higher primates, such as baboons, have red, hairless skin on the buttocks which they present to other members of their troop as an appeasement display. The buttocks area of the female becomes redder when she is in oestrus. This visual display, together with a change in the odour that she releases as a vaginal secretion, attracts the male and stimulates sexual behaviour (see also Chapter Four on olfactory signals).

Evolution of vocal communication

So far, we have discussed examples illustrating evolutionary processes that might have been involved in visual displays but we have made only passing reference to the evolution of vocal communication and its associated auditory perception.

We must emphasise that vocal signals are usually accompanied by visual signals, sometimes quite elaborate and sometimes merely the postures that the animal must adopt in order to produce the vocalisation. In evolutionary terms these two aspects of signalling are intimately linked. Unfortunately, researchers studying communication tend to concentrate on only one aspect of the signal pattern (usually either visual or vocal) and this limits our understanding of the entire signalling 'package'. This is particularly so in the study of vocal communication—the vocal signals have been described in great detail with very little attention to the accompanying visual signals. We suggest two reasons for this. The first reason might be the available technology for studying communication: whereas it was easy to take a high-quality tape recorder into the field to record the vocalisations of animals, video records of animal postures were, until recently, made difficult by cumbersome recording equipment and often impossible by not being in direct sight of the subject.

The other reason for the focus on sound has been the drive to understand the vocal communication of animals, particularly primates, in order to understand the evolution of human language. This focus on language has led many researchers to ignore anything other than the sounds made. If there has been any broader perspective than this, it has been to consider the gestures that primates make with their hands and, on this basis, some researchers (e.g. Gordon Hewes (1973) of the University of Colorado) have considered the possibility that human language may have evolved from the gestures of primates. Communication by voice and hands are human forms of communication. There has been little attention, however, to communication in primates by eye movements, odours, breathing patterns or ear movements, any of which—alone or in combination—could have laid a basis for the evolution of human language.

It is not our aim to cover the evolution of human language here, but we remind the reader of the apes taught to use sign and symbolic language to communicate with humans (Chapters Two and Four) and, in particular, of Kanzi's ability to understand the syntax of English (Chapter Two). There are other characteristics of animals' ability to process sounds that are shared with humans and considered to be essential for language. These include the ability to control vocalisations and to use them referentially (Chapters Two and Four), and the ability to perceive sounds categorically, as we explain next.

Categorical perception is the ability to perceive sounds in categories that are discrete from one another, even though the variation in sound is actually continuous. The receiver parcels the auditory information so that it is in categories rather than a continuous stream of variation. For example, humans can hear the difference between 'da' and 'ta' sounds without any difficulty. If we use a computer to generate a range of sounds from 'da' to 'ta' so that there is a continuous gradation from one to the other and then we play these to a human subject, subjects will say they heard a collection of 'das' and 'tas' but not a continuum. Our perception creates a boundary between the two sounds that makes us believe there is a far more abrupt transition from 'da' to 'ta' than actually exists. We categorise the sounds and this is said to be an important ability in understanding speech sounds. Not surprisingly, it was thought that the ability to categorise sounds was uniquely human. We now know that that is not so. As we saw in Chapter Four, May, Moody and Stebbins (1989), of the University of Michigan, have shown that Japanese macaque monkeys (*Macaca fuscata*) have categorical perception. The researchers selected two calls that the monkeys make when they want to establish contact with each other, one with a peak in frequency (pitch) early in the call and the other with a peak later in the call. From these they synthesised a range of calls, grading one into the other, and tested the monkeys with them to see whether they could distinguish one call from another. The researchers found that, although the monkeys were presented with a continuous gradation of calls, they perceived them as falling into two distinct categories, showing that the monkeys have categorical perception.

Categorical perception has also been demonstrated in chinchillas, who were tested with speech sounds; moreover, the boundary between one category and another found in chinchillas was the same as that in humans. Even Japanese quail categorise speech sounds and a range of avian and primate species hear their own species calls categorically. There is now no question that this aspect of perception is shared by animals and humans (Kuhl 1988).

The same is true of another aspect of vocal processing once thought to be unique to humans—lateralisation, the processing of speech sounds and the production of speech by the left, and not the right, hemisphere of the brain. For many years it had been thought that the specialisation of the left hemisphere for speech and language processing was a characteristic unique to humans and a mark of our superiority over all other species. As reviewed by John Bradshaw and Lesley Rogers (1993), there is now conclusive evidence that many species, including monkeys, mice, birds and frogs, process or produce the vocalisations of their own species using only the left side of the brain. This attribute of the brain also evolved very early, contrary to beliefs once held.

Despite these similarities in auditory processing across so many different species, there are, of course, differences between species in auditory perception and vocal production. These differences are determined by auditory experience, learning and evolutionary processes. We will discuss some of these evolutionary differences briefly. We have seen already that bats can hear sounds that we do not and that they use these ultrasounds both to communicate and to signal (Chapter Four). As in the case of vision, the hearing ranges of species vary and they have evolved to match the transmission properties of the environment in which each species lives.

The evolution of birdsong has been considered by many scientists. Why have the songs of birds become so complex? In Chapter One, we discussed the experiments in which

John Krebs played back songs of European great tits in the field and found that the larger the song repertoire that he played through the loudspeaker the more effectively birds were kept out of the area surrounding the speaker. The more complex the song, the better it is at advertising that the bird holds a territory. This is a plausible reason why more complex songs evolved. There is also some evidence that females prefer to mate with males with more complex songs and this too would provide a means by which song complexity would evolve. It also provides a reason why the learning required to perform complex songs takes place.

Dialects of birdsong, regional variations among the members of one species, have been a source of speculation about the evolution of song but, so far, evidence is lacking that there is any link between song dialect and genetic differences. We will avoid further speculation on this topic while referring the reader to the book on birdsong by Clive Catchpole and Peter Slater (1995) (Chapter Nine).

Conclusion

The evolution of communication is a topic that has attracted the attention of ethologists and anthropologists. There has been much speculation and some testable hypotheses. At this time, however, it is not a field in which we can isolate definite facts. This is partly due to the intangibility of evolutionary processes by direct experimentation. We cannot go back in time to sample the potential effects of genes of extinct species and, more particularly, we cannot observe the behaviour of extinct species. Behaviour does not leave a fossil record. Therefore, we can only attempt to piece together the jigsaw of the evolution of communication by observing the signals and displays of existing species and design experiments to test hypotheses on these species.

The other problem with general, broad-sweeping hypotheses about evolutionary processes is that they do not take into account the enormous variation in species. All too often, the results obtained by testing a single species are extrapolated to explain what happens for all species. This is acceptable as a starting point to understanding, and we have been guilty of doing this ourselves, but every hypothesis needs to be tested on a range of species in a range of testing environments. That is the challenge and a multitude of exciting experiments lie ahead in this area of the study of communication.

To end this chapter, we urge caution when considering hypotheses that tie complex behaviour and brain function to unitary genetic causes no matter how neat they appear on the surface.

CHAPTER SEVEN

HUMAN–ANIMAL CONTACTS

Human–animal contacts have many different contexts and take a variety of forms. Without question, human attitudes to animals play a significant role in the way we treat them, in the freedom we accord them and in the manner in which we are willing to learn about their own worlds and lives. Now, more than ever, we need to learn more about animals and more about our attitudes to animals. The latter will finally decide whether many species will have a future. Many human–animal encounters are not favourable for animals. Indeed, some contact with animals exists solely for the purpose of destroying animals in mass production and consumption.

There is another side, however, the only one in which communication really plays a role, and that is contact between humans and animals in work or as companions. These relationships can become very significant for us and possibly also for the animal. The dog, in particular, has been of great importance to humans for at least 12 000 years. Animals bond with humans and many humans bond with their pets. Two to three thousand years ago, such a bond might have lasted for the best part of human life. In Roman times (BC) the human lifespan was about 24 years and presumably domesticated animals might have had similar lifespans as now. Today, of course, humans have extended their lifespan so significantly that pet owners tend to have serial relationships with dogs and cats.

Domestication extended to goats and sheep about 9000 years ago, followed by cattle and pigs and, in some areas, the horse (about 5000 years ago). The sheer passage of time makes us wonder how far domesticated species have changed as a result of becoming captives of human society. As Jonica Newby (1997) pointed out, most domesticated animals have never attained the status of closeness as dogs and cats have.

Human–animal relationships have not remained static through the ages, yet their history remains largely unwritten, with some notable exceptions, as for instance in works published by James Serpell (1995, 1996) and by Aubrey Manning (1994). Only recently has welfare become an issue. Despite some significant forerunners as far back as the 18th and 19th centuries, many societies have begun only in the last few decades seriously and consistently to address the ethical issues involved in all aspects of animal life and animal management and control.

Mythology of animals

We begin with an unusual perspective of the human–animal relationship—namely, with fairy-tales and popular mythology. Why raise this in a book on animal communication? First, fairy-tales and myths about animals abound in all cultures and we might well read from them what a society desires or fears. In fairy-tales, musicals and fables, human creativity has always expressed its desire, if not its yearning, to understand what animals say and mean. Dr Doolittle, for instance, thinks of animal communication as language that we have simply failed to learn but can still learn. Second, animal communication is firmly embedded in the cultural records of many cultures. Finally, the manner in which fairy-tales and mythology deal with animals—and herein lies our interest—might well mould the attitude of the young to animals which, in turn, might influence the kind of relationship they will have with animals in their wown lives. For instance, German fairy-tales involving animals tend to be romantic and, as we see later in this chapter, recent surveys have shown that the Germans hold largely positive and often romantic attitudes towards animals. Whether modern attitudes are a consequence of childhood education, including romantic fairy-tales about animals, or unrelated to such exposure is a question that we cannot answer here.

Unlike the science of animal communication, which continually highlights our difficulties in attributing reasonable explanations to acts of animal signalling, the wonderful aspect of fairy-tales is that everything in the story happens effortlessly and by design. As is well known, animals feature in most fairy-tales but not always in the role of communicators. There are stories, however, that focus our attention on animal communication. We cannot do more here than point to a few examples in a very rich field.

Perhaps one of the most interesting stories we know in which human and animal worlds overlap is the fairy-tale by Wilhelm Hauff, called *Mutabor*. Hauff was a writer of the romantic period (1802–27). Hauff's tales are set in the era of Harun al-Rashid, a legendary ruler of Baghdad. We relate this story in some detail because it illustrates what assumptions we make about animals when speaking of animal communication.

In the setting of a collection of fairy-tales, a travelling group of businessmen tell each other stories, slowly making their way with camels through the desert. The story, *Mutabor*, is one of the most famous. Here, an evil magician wishes to get the sultan out of the way and, via a trader, offers the sultan a powder in a box with a Latin inscription. The inscription says that anyone sniffing this powder will turn into the animal he sees when turning towards Mecca and speaking the word 'Mutabor'. The sultan and his adviser promptly try this and turn into storks, as there are some storks in sight. Both men can now understand what the storks are saying. The inscription also says that one condition for their return to human stature is that they must never laugh while they are in animal form. If they do, they will forget the word 'Mutabor' and remain animals forever. However, on understanding what the storks are saying, both men are promptly very amused by a young female stork who is practising a dance performance. They laugh heartily at what they perceive as a clumsy attempt at dancing. They are now caught in stork garb and find it difficult to adjust, particularly to the food, although they like their new ability of flight.

The story leads us to a sad owl, crying tears in a distant palace. She is actually a princess who was turned into an owl when she refused the hand of the evil magician's son. She can only be freed if someone proposes marriage to her while she is still an owl. The sultan/stork, a bachelor of many years, offers his hand in marriage and she, still an owl, leads them to the place where the magician always meets his supporters. There they hear the word 'Mutabor' and can now change back into human form. The owl is transformed into a beautiful young girl and the sultan returns to his rightful place in society as a just and celebrated man.

There are several aspects of this story worth noting. First, natural curiosity drove the sultan and his adviser to sniff the powder despite the risks involved. We can assume that they were interested in knowing what animals had to say to each other. Second, they thoroughly enjoyed understanding the society of the stork. The third assumption is that 'stork language' translates into that of another animal species (here the owl), and the fourth assumption is that the sultan is a better man as a result of his experiences as an animal. He has certainly been enriched and the wife he could not find in human form he found when he was an animal. On the other hand, capturing someone in animal form is obviously meant to be a punishment. The owl/girl cried because of the loneliness and the night she has to endure. The pivotal point of the story is how and when they would rediscover the magic word that would return them to human form. It was also made clear that the characters retained their identities as sultan and adviser, even as storks. Only the bodies had changed, not the minds.

One of the most telling parts of the story, and this is why it has been told here in detail, is that the evil magician predicted very accurately that both the sultan and his adviser would laugh once they were turned into animals. And of course the reader is equally taken into the plot. Would we think that it is easy not to laugh? Or would we think, like the magician, that animal behaviour is ridiculous or amusing and therefore inevitably it would make us laugh? The story works only if it is assumed that laughter is inevitable.

The story also betrays the early ethologist. Neither man actually enters the society of storks; they just eavesdrop on their conversation. Interestingly, by changing form they become 'bilingual'. They could still understand human language but they also understood the animals. By deduction this might also mean that animals can understand us even though we cannot understand them.

In other tales, animals are used purely symbolically. There is evidence from the earliest written records that animals have long been used to describe human society. In many stories—from parables to fairy-tales to modern comic strips (thinking of the many Walt Disney animal movies and animal cartoons)—there is an assumption that animals can either demonstrate human nature well or that animals have societies like humans and it is only a matter of unlocking the doors to these secret worlds. Walt Disney's animal figures aside, the film *Babe* has been highly successful, with animals walking and talking, forming societies, suffering pain and loss, feeling pride and, most of all, maintaining a system of communication not unlike ours. They are made to be like us. It is culturally a very Australian story: Babe is the little battler who has to use his honesty and ingenuity to deserve a place in the life of the farm without getting killed and eaten. In *Watership Down* and George Orwell's *Animal Farm*, animals speak as a parable for human qualities and, often, animals are chosen to conceal the political intent behind the tale.

Ancient Greek fables (by Aesop) attribute specific characteristics to certain animals: there is the clever/cunning fox, the rapacious wolf, the deceitful snake, the dignified lion, the plotting tiger, the innocent sheep. In 2000 years of Western image making, these 'characters' have remained stock-in-trade stereotypes of behaviours the basis of which is very dubious. In Irish folk-tales, animals are often cruel and deceptive towards each other and they often involve a fox. There is a European magpie outwitting a fox and killing him. There is an eagle who gets betrayed by a crow. Interestingly, fairy-tales from China and other Asian countries often show an entirely different relationship to animals. Here, the origin of the animal may become the pivotal point for the tale. For instance, in Chinese folk-tales the ox is originally a heavenly creature. The emperor of heaven took pity on people and allowed the ox to descend to earth to help them. In other versions there is Ti-sang P'usa, the 'fallen' deity who inhabits hell as a consequence of becoming the guarantor for the human species, promising Yü huang-ti (the highest deity in popular religion) that human beings are going to be good to animals. With that guarantee, Yühuang-ti permits the sending of the ox to help the people plough the field but as the ox grew older, they killed it, skinned and ate it. Ti-sang P'usa had promised that he would go to hell if humans did these things. Hence Ti-sang P'usa went to hell and was allowed to open his eyes only on the thirtieth day of the seventh month. In some regions, incense was lit in commemoration of the services of Ti-sang P'usa to humanity.

In many fairy-tales and myths there is an added sexual element embedded in the animal–human relationship which may take different forms. It would take us too far away from animal communication to debate these but closeness or revulsion to animals has been exploited in stories with subtle sexual overtones. In stories told by the indigenous peoples of Borneo, which we detail in our book on orang-utans, we found a number of examples where orang-utans and humans intermarried and had children (Kaplan & Rogers 1995). 'Orang' means 'man' or human. Hence there are some languages and some cultures in which the division of human and animal is not necessarily expressed linguistically and may not exist in the mind. 'Orang-utan' means man of the forest. The local tribespeople also refer to each other as orang-utan (man of the forest) and orang-sungai (man of the river). The breakdown of the human–animal divide in these indigenous stories also leads to unimpeded communication between humans and orang-utans, and possibly to respect of orang-utans.

Respect for animals happens all too rarely but it is probably a precondition for good communication with animals. There are human cultures into which respect for (some) animals is inbuilt. For instance, in the Hindu religion humans are said to pass from one life form to another. The same human being may have been reincarnated as several animals before taking human form. Australian Aboriginal cultures have a deep link with the physical world. On the day when conception of a new child is thought to have happened (not at birth, which is not a greatly celebrated event in traditional Aboriginal culture), the child to be born is inextricably linked to an animal or a tree or a rock in situ. It is the presence of a lizard during conception that will give the child a lizard spirit. No doubt, such spiritual links can significantly alter the perception of animals by people holding beliefs of this kind.

When we speak here of human–animal contacts we are limited to observations in the western world

- because the Western world has little direct access to the cultures that have chosen very different relationships to animals,
- Western attitudes dominate most of the world's natural resources as well as its flora and fauna, and
- coupled with our Western attitudes is a Judaeo-Christian tradition that invites humans to be masters of all the earth—a strategic blueprint that has been followed unfailingly.

Histories of human–animal relationships

There are anecdotal stories and myths about animals that are alleged to have reared humans. Occasionally, we hear of so-called feral children who are supposed to have been reared by wild animals. There is, for instance, the myth of Romulus and Remus, the founders of Rome, who were allegedly nourished by a wolf bitch. Then there is the story of a boy, Tarzan, who was described as growing up with apes. Other famous stories of feral children include Kaspar Hauser, that of the Wild Boy of Aveyron and, more recently, of the Indian children Kamala, Amala and Ramu. There was also a boy reared by deer, who is said to have used his hands to imitate the movement of ears for communicative purposes. Douglas Candland's book on feral children (1993) provides fascinating examples.

Unfortunately, in modern cases in which children were thought to have been raised by animals, the basis of that assumption was that the human child or juvenile showed no mastery of human speech. The public interest these cases created was for the sake of documenting the development of the human capacity for speech rather than the communication and actual experiences of the person growing up in isolation from humans. Steven Pinker (1994) from MIT is right in suggesting that most of the stories are mythology. In reality, these children might have been locked away in rooms, deprived of speech and communication rather than reared by animals. (We mentioned the documented case of Genie in Chapter Five.) These instances, therefore, tell us little about animal–human contacts and communication.

Animal–human attitudes are located somewhere, and sometimes implicitly, within the discourse concerned with Western views of nature. Within this we may narrow the parameters to look at specific relationships of human societies in the past. Human contacts that might at first have been exclusively with wild animals could be compared with those contacts that have brought humans and animals into closer proximity through the process of domestication of animals. Domestication has been defined by Juliet Clutton-Brock (1994) from the Natural History Museum, London, as a process by which an animal is bred in captivity for purposes of subsistence or profit, and by which that animal lives in a human community that maintains complete mastery over its breeding, organisation of territory and food supply.

Juliet Clutton-Brock and other researchers in the field distinguish 'domestication' from 'taming' and this is a useful distinction in so far as taming may involve companionship. Taming may involve both humans and animals in work or leisure but may well exclude the final elements of domestication—targeting animals for slaughter. In both processes, the domestic or tamed animal is rightly regarded as a cultural artefact of human society. This is a very recent phenomenon in natural history. Domestication or taming thus signals a substantial change in the relationship of one species to another. We know of few examples in the natural world where one species is kept to provide a livelihood for another, although cases of symbiosis between two species do exist. There are also some insects, ants for instance, that have utilised other species of insects to provide them with continued sustenance, but these examples are extremely rare. Only the human species has insisted continually on subjugating other species to its will.

In social histories, domestication of animals has been treated as a watershed in human progress. In many accounts, Tim Ingold (1994) rightly claims, the domestication of animals signals nothing less than the beginnings of 'civilisedness'. Perceptions of human progress are thus intrinsically tied to the subjugation of animals. Clearly, to view human progress in this light and to accord domestication of animals the status of a giant leap in the organisation of human society leaves some human groups behind—namely, those groups that did not domesticate animals, the hunters and gatherers, and even those who did not settle down, the nomads. Ingold argues that, from the

19th century onwards, only those who produced their own food were regarded as fully human. Hunting and gathering, or foraging, was considered little better than the life of an animal because this is precisely what animals do. They hunt and gather just enough for their own immediate needs and those of their offspring. Inferiority and superiority of human and animal societies could therefore be decided on methods of gathering food. Subsistence was inferior and surplus superior.

However, our views of hunter–gatherer societies have changed markedly in the last two to three decades, because more objective studies have revealed that hunter–gatherer societies were not 'primitive' in the way Darwin saw them. Nor are (or were) they wretched people at the point of starvation and lawlessness. Indeed, some influential papers of the early 1970s showed that tribal society was often an affluent society, without disease or immediate survival pressures. Moreover, the knowledge of hunter–gatherers about the behaviour of animals, their sounds and their habits was intimate. Only in this way could they hunt them successfully. That intimate relationship was not, as it is now, one of antagonism, hate, control or domination but one of conservation.

The idea of domestication of animals arose in nomadic societies that kept stock. But the idea of domination of nature evolved in stationary societies that learnt to plough fields and used domesticated animals to help them in their work and exploited them for their meat and other products on a planned, regular basis. Nevertheless, the simple paradigm that agriculture and farming need to lead to antagonism and animal exploitation is not entirely valid. The Boisi, a group of farming people in India, have followed ecological principles for many centuries and have created a small and stable community on the principle of living with nature rather than against it. Meat eating in this society is strictly prohibited.

As long as human groups were relatively small and the livelihood of the people depended entirely on the flocks or herds they held, it is often possible to observe some substantial involvement with the domesticated animals. For instance, cormorants are still used in some South East Asian countries, chiefly Indonesia and Japan, to help their owners catch fish. Monkeys are used to pick coconuts, dogs for hunting game and foxes, and pigeons may relay messages. In Mongolia to this day deer are the most cherished (and often the only) possession and the people's relationship to the deer is embedded in mythology even to the point of associating their stock with their gods. Very often these ancient working relationships have been positive one-to-one relationships between humans and animals. The owners not only worked with them but slept with them. They shared each other's food and their family life. A good owner of such an animal would be identifiable by the animal staying close to him or her (without restraint) after the work is done, relaxing and sleeping.

To get animals to do our work, there must be at least a degree of training and communication. Why else would animals, especially those that are much larger and stronger than humans, obey the whims of their owner or carer? In the last century in Thailand, elephants were taken to battle with neighbouring countries and, today, some elephants still work in the timber industry as a mode of transport. Foremost in Thailand, but also in Malaysia and India, there are still training schools for elephants. Each trainer spends a good deal of time with his elephant and each elephant is teamed up with an older and more experienced elephant. Training may take up to two years. In that time the elephants learn to respond to verbal commands and requests. It is possible to achieve a level of cooperation that requires no threats of punishment and not even food rewards. In the forests of southern and South East Asia, rider and elephant are often on their own. Trainer and trainee learn to trust each other through experience, consistency and, not least, through effective communication. Such communication cannot just work one way, from trainer to trainee. Some of it must also go the other way.

The trainer must understand the ways of an elephant and must be able to read the elephant's signals appropriately. A trainer who does not understand when an elephant expresses anger may have a very short life.

The water buffalo ploughs the fields in Asia, still linked with his human master by the plough. Most of the peoples in the Middle East rely on the camel for personal transport and the transport of goods; they tend to care well for them because ultimately their own lives are linked with those of their animals.

We do not want to romanticise relationships with animals that are built on their removal from a life of freedom and with their own kind and that are, at times, subject to outright exploitation. What needs to be said, however, is that in these intimate forms of work relationships, the level of communication with the animal is often better than that between pet and pet owner. Mutual reliance can occur only with good communication.

War on animals

The Industrial Revolution in Europe probably did more to change our thinking about the non-human environment than any other single set of events. Production could be driven to new heights and its main parameters were based on the ideas of specialisation and overproduction (i.e. producing more than is needed for one's own survival). These attitudes were transferred to the non-human environment. Taking from nature whatever was necessary for sustaining a never-satisfied desire for more goods and objects turned our relationship with the natural environment into one not just of alienation but of exploitation. Every forest, every patch of water and plot of land has since been viewed with an eye on the price it could fetch. Domination and exploitation of this kind required a change in attitude towards animals. The hunter may have admired the strength, shape or intelligence of an animal but this changed with the development of industry which raised animals on a mass scale for the purpose of consuming them. They were kept in confinement until they were ready for the killing. Knowledge about animals and their behaviour was no longer relevant unless it affected production. Nor was respect of animals and their world at all necessary in this kind of relationship between humans and animals. Such developments can be traced readily in the imagery of travelogues, movies and popular accounts over the last 150 years and it is noticeable, as we found when we researched the imagery of orang-utans in such source materials, that modern attitudes vary between fear and indifference, but never include respect (Kaplan 1995).

In the second half of the 20th century, we are encountering additional ethical problems as genetic engineering pushes arguments about the rights of animals to new limits, as Colin Tudge (1993) debated a few years ago. Do animals have the right to remain untampered with genetically? 'Designer' animals are bred to provide 'spare parts' of living tissue for humans. The image of the mouse carrying an unfurred human-shaped ear on its back may be bizarre but it symbolises a new, and this time grotesquely visible, peak in animal exploitation. Cloned animals are now also a reality. The principles of healthy biodiversity have been thrown to the wind because these animals are, after all, 'made' for human consumption. Needless to say, historically these new activities present the lowest point in human–animal relationships. Simultaneously, however, there have been strong counterforces, concerned with the ethical issues of farming on one hand and the conservation issues of wildlife on the other. Even mainstream thinking in Western societies had to admit that our management of the natural world has visibly led to an avalanche of extinctions of vast numbers of species—mammalian, reptilian, avian and invertebrate—and that this may ultimately affect our quality of life as well.

As a species, we have interfered and killed too much, thought too little and wondered too little about the consequences of our actions. Now there are conservation societies, wildlife protection societies, animal liberation societies and projects that show the alarmed concern of some. The Great Ape Project, for instance, is a plea for the rights of apes as our closest relatives in evolutionary terms. Animal protection societies and societies for the prevention of cruelty to animals have impressively large numbers of members. Yet the slide towards extinction continues for many species because they have 'products' that some want and will pay high prices to obtain, such as the ivory of elephants, the skin and teeth of tigers, the horn of rhinoceroses, the live bodies of apes for pets, zoos and circuses, the whale meat for speciality restaurants and many other species, such as birds, for our amusement. Others, such as the orang-utan, are marked to vanish from this earth because of our requirement of space for agriculture, mining and forest timber, which we take from their natural habitat. The national parks and wildlife reserves that have been steadily created throughout this century have often been isolated areas and they usually occupy less than one per cent of the area within the political boundary of a nation, too small in the long run to sustain diversity and too small to sustain healthy populations.

Only a few species have genuinely benefited from expanding human habitation and these are mostly species that are not popular, such as invertebrates (especially cockroaches), rodents (mice and rats) and opossums and squirrels. Among bird species, there are the sparrows, the crows and the pigeons. Many of these are treated as vermin. In cities, especially in industrialised countries, tolerance for animals, including insects, in close vicinity has dramatically declined. Household sprays and rodent poisons feature high in human consumption. Pesticide spraying is often higher in cities than in primary producing rural areas. In homes, gardens, streets and public spaces, the human inhabitants have declared war on all the remnants of living things. The very same people may then keep a pet. This is only seemingly a contradiction. What it indicates is that in modern urban contexts, in particular, humans expect to have total control over animals and to make decisions about what species can coexist with them at any time.

In industrialised countries, chiefly Europe and Japan, the idea of total control has long since been extended to the broader landscape. The dichotomy between rural and urban no longer really exists in many of these countries because wilderness has disappeared entirely. Both Europe and Japan have highly managed landscapes. As Stephen Kellert (1994) points out, this is because a lengthy history of human settlement and land use has made many indigenous species disappear entirely or they are currently being maintained in very regulated and controlled circumstances. Nelsen (1987) notes, too, that the Germans have so regulated their forests that game management has become artificial and simplified to the extent that the average German is removed from direct contact with or responsibility for wildlife.

The same holds true for Japan. Japan today has a noticeable absence of animals. Few people keep pets, although there is a brisk trade in expensive exotic pets, and there are very few places where animals are kept in fields. Kellert's study of attitudes to wildlife in the industrial superpowers is revealing. Germans appear to have romantic notions of wildlife and nature, but it is wildlife that is no longer there for them to see, unless they travel to distant places on the globe. Japanese, by contrast, according to Kellert, have less knowledge of animals and more negative attitudes to them than were found in Germany and the United States. On the island of Hokkaido, the most northern main island of Japan, there is a bear farm displaying the remnants of an indigenous bear population in unpleasant and crowded conditions. On the same property, there are bears performing circus tricks and opposite this arena there is a shopping complex selling bear-paw ashtrays, fake bear feet, bear teeth chains and other bear trinkets. The contradictions in this bear farm are apparently not obvious to the management or visitors. Part of the history of human–animal relationships is a dismal story of the destruction of human–animal coexistence.

Positive bonds and the benefits of animals

Despite the bleak imagery that can be drawn in this century of ecological crisis, there remain attempts to try to coexist and to see value in animals beyond killing them for their produce. In laboratories, in research stations and on some farms, there are attempts to give animals better living conditions. Some people have started to acknowledge that animals have preferences, interests and needs beyond physical survival. Marian Dawkins (1993) argues for giving animals choices in the selection of their environment. Why not ask them? This view is not only dependent on a human attitude of respect for an animal, it also accepts that animals can tell us something—that is, effectively communicate with us. Many people keep pets and here communication may work relatively well because of a preselected history of species. First, we tend to choose species with communication systems that fall largely into our own range of perception. We may not hear as well as dogs or see as well as cats in the dark, we do not have the same colour perception as birds but we can hear them, see them, touch them and speak to them. And, second, when we do get close to our pets we usually claim to understand them. Our pets train us as much as we are supposed to train them. We learn to respond to their wishes to leave the room or the house, we seem to be perfectly aware when they want to be near us, want affection, attention or simply their food. We can understand some of their signals and they understand ours.

Beyond our desire to share our private lives with pets, many industrial societies have now also designed programs in which animals are used, but for more benign purposes than in the past. Boris Levinson (1969) discovered the great advantages of companion animals in clinical psychology and medicine. Research has since been done to show that animals can reduce stress in humans, that companion animals can increase self-esteem and, even more dramatically, can lower levels of accepted risk factors for cardiovascular disease (Blackshaw 1996).

Interestingly, the new 'uses' of animals are often related to communication and the senses. This is a relatively new field of study and practice. A recent study showed that dogs can identify matching human body scents in 80 per cent of cases. A dog's olfactory sensitivity, selectivity and memory, as well as its capacity for odour pattern recognition, is used in criminal investigations and security operations. Settle (1994) predicts that these skills are unlikely to be challenged by any artificial sensor in the foreseeable future. The literature today also refers to a 'human–companion animal bond'. There are now programs in place throughout the Western world which have placed the human–animal bond on a new footing. Pet Facilitated Psychotherapy is one such program. Better known are the Pets as Therapy programs and Guide Dogs for the Blind. There are also Hearing Dogs for the Deaf. A study by Guttman, Pedrovic and Zemanek in 1985 found that children who have pets not only have greater self-esteem but they are also better in non-verbal communication. Hart, Hart and Bergin (1987) argue that impaired people in wheelchairs, in any of the health programs with pets, tend to smile more, are greeted more often and engage in conversation to a much greater extent than wheelchaired people without pets. Pets are thus regarded as great facilitators in communication among humans and there are perceived benefits for humans in keeping pets, whether as a symbiosis (cats dealing with vermin or dogs protecting the home) or for companionship.

Relatively little is said about the actual communication between animal and human, or the quality of life that these animals are afforded. In an industrial context that is anti-animal, it is often difficult to develop attitudes that have the interest of the animal at heart, let alone the willingness to communicate with animals. On many occasions, communication with animals may be sought but it is not always welcome. One of the most astounding realisations to many people has been that not all animals feel privileged to be singled out for human attention. In today's world, most wild animals are afraid of humans. They have cause to be. For those of us who rehabilitate wildlife there is a further realisation, sometimes quite shocking, that animals, when left alone, do not need or want us at all. The best service we can do them is to leave them alone and leave them with the appropriate habitat in which they can thrive, if we can still do that. Arnold Arluke (1994) describes these as the modern contradictions of our relationship with animals, showering them with affection at one end of the spectrum while simultaneously maltreating and killing them as utilitarian objects.

Conclusion

Darwin, and subsequently the works of the 20th century, has bequeathed to us several substantial problems and issues in our relationship with animals. First, we were told that animals in some way or another are our evolutionary ancestors. This century, many have fought hard to dispel this notion of continuity with animals at the same time as pretending that the Darwinian model is acceptable as a plausible scientific model for the development of life on earth. Within that model there continued to be emphasis on upholding the 'uniquenesses' of human beings as the pinnacle of creation. These categorical distinctions have begun to be broken down, whether in studies on brain asymmetry, tool use, problem solving, sensory perception, learning or other categories that were previously used as markers of unique human qualities.

The communication system is one of the chief categories constructed in the distinction between humans and animals. Controversy has raged this century about the possibility of animals having a language-like system of communication, and about the possibility of animals communicating effectively with humans on human language terms. Roitblat, Harley and Helweg (1993) rightly point out that little work in psychology has engendered as much emotional involvement and heated argument as research into animal 'language'.

Throughout this book we have referred to research that has put its energy into training dolphins, apes and birds to acquire sufficient communication skills (either as vocalisations or as symbols or sign language) for us to communicate across the species divide and learn more about the possibility of consciousness in animals, their ability to use past events or ponder future possibilities. These training and communication efforts have shown extreme dedication on the part of individual humans, involving often a lifetime of work, and a gracious indulgence on the part of the trained animal who, after all, was entirely deprived of any of its natural life alternatives and often also of same-species companionship. Together humans and animals have lived and grown to explore the possibilities of meaningful communication across human/animal borders and to answer perhaps some of the questions about the extent of similarities and differences between humans and some animals. The interest in doing so has many sources and probably many intellectual justifications. One of the most relevant is the desire to learn more about the evolution of linguistic competencies. We cannot study this from fossil records because communication, for all its vitality and importance, leaves no trace.

We have referred equally in this book to studies that have placed animals in close proximity to humans (the laboratory or even the home) as well as those that have studied animal communication in the natural setting. Charles Snowdon (1993) from the University of Wisconsin has called ethologists 'cross-species anthropologists'. It is only in the natural environment that answers to a number of questions concerned with communication will be answered. For instance, as Snowdon argues, the linguistic ethologist may ask about the evolutionary precursors of various linguistic phenomena:

- What are the environmental conditions that might have led to symbolic communication?
- What are the circumstances that lead to syntactic structures?
- What developmental influences affect the acquisition of phonology, comprehension or usage?

In this field, it needs to be asked whether an emphasis on vocal and hence linguistic development is adequate. As we have seen, communication systems are complex and may involve several senses at once, some of which the human observer is only capable of studying by developing techno-logical aids for their detection. Equipped with the naked eye or ear and our sense of smell alone, we would never have discovered the diversity and complexity of animal communication, as far as we know it today.

At the close of the 20th century, researchers from very different fields and with very different agendas may agree that the study of animal communication, and the discovery of commonalities of some aspects of communication across species, raises the possibility of viewing human language as one of several alternative systems of communication. Never before in human history has there been such intense engagement with animals in a scientific manner in trying to understand how they communicate with each other and how they may communicate with humans. Never before has there been such an urgent need to do so.

FURTHER READING

Chapter One   What is communication?

Blest, A.D. (1957) The function of eyespot patterns in the lepidoptera. *Behaviour*, 11, 209–256.

Brindley, E.L. (1991) Response of European robins to playback of song: neighbour recognition and overlapping. *Animal Behaviour*, 41, 503–512.

Bullock, T.H. & Heiligenberg, W. (1986) *Electroreception*. Wiley & Sons, New York.

Caro, T.M. (1995) Pursuit-deterrence revisited. *TREE*, 10, 500–503.

Cheney, D.L. & Seyfarth, R.M. (1990) *How Monkeys See the World: Inside the Mind of Another Species*. University of Chicago Press, Chicago.

Cullen, J.M. (1972) Some principles of animal communication. In R.A. Hinde (ed.) *Non-verbal Communication*. Cambridge University Press, Cambridge, pp. 101–122.

Eibl-Eibesfeldt, I. (1972) Similarities and differences between cultures in expressive movements. In R.A. Hinde (ed.) *Non-verbal Communication*, Cambridge University Press, Cambridge, pp. 297–314.

Endler, J.A. (1993) The color of light in forests and its implications. *Ecological Monographs*, 63(1), 1–27.

Evans, C.S. & Marler, P. (1991) On the use of video images as social stimuli in birds: audience effects on alarm calling. *Animal Behaviour*, 41, 17–26.

Evans, C.S., Evans, L. & Marler, P. (1993) On the meaning of alarm calls: functional reference in an avian vocal system. *Animal Behaviour*, 46, 23–38.

Hauser, M.D. (1996) *The Evolution of Communication*. MIT Press, Cambridge, Mass.

Huxley, J.S. (1914) The courtship habits of the great crested grebe (*Podiceps cristatus*); with an addition on the theory of sexual selection. *Proceedings of the Zoological Society of London*, 35, 491–562.

Jolly, A. (1966) *Lemur Behavior*. University of Chicago Press, Chicago.

Krebs, J.R. (1977) Song and territory in the great tit *Parus major*. In B. Stonehouse & C. Perrins (eds) *Evolutionary Ecology*. Macmillan, London, pp. 47–62.

Krebs, J.R., Ashcroft, R. & Webber, M. (1978) Song repertoires and territory defence in the great tit. *Nature*, 271, 539–542.

Kroodsma, D.E. (1990) Using appropriate experimental designs for intended hypotheses in 'song' playbacks, with examples of testing effects of song repertoire sizes. *Animal Behaviour*, 40, 1138–1150.

Leal, M. & Rodriguez, J.A. (1997) Signalling displays during predator-prey interactions in a Puerto Rican anole, Anolis cristatellus. *Animal Behaviour*, 54, 1147–1154.

Macedonia, J.M., Evans, C.S. & Losos, J.B. (1994) Male *Anolis* lizards discriminate video-recorded conspecific and heterospecific displays. *Animal Behaviour*, 47, 1220–1223.

Randall, J.A. (1997) Species-specific foot-drumming in kangaroo rats: *Dipodomys ingens, D. desertii, D. spectabilis*. *Animal Behaviour*, 54, 1167–1175.

Seyfarth, R.M., Cheney, D.L. & Marler, P. (1980) Vervet monkey alarm calls: semantic communication in a free-ranging primate. *Animal Behaviour*, 28, 1070–1094.

Shanas, U. & Terkel, J. (1997) Mole-rat harderian gland secretions inhibit aggression. *Animal Behaviour*, 54, 1255–1263.

Stoddart, D.M. (1990) *The Scented Ape*. Cambridge University Press, Cambridge.

Chapter Two   Signalling

Blumstein, D.T. & Armitage, K.B. (1997) Alarm calling in yellow-bellied marmots: I. The meaning of situationally variable alarm calls. *Animal Behaviour*, 53, 143–171.

Byrne, R. (1995) *The Thinking Ape: The Evolutionary Origins of Intelligence*. Oxford University Press, Oxford.

Cheney, D.L. & Seyfarth, R.M. (1985) Vervet monkey alarm calls: manipulation through shared information? *Behaviour*, 94, 150–166.

——(1990) *How Monkeys See the World: Inside the Mind of Another Species*. University of Chicago Press, Chicago.

Dawkins, M.S. (1993) *Through Our Eyes Only? The Search for Animal Consciousness*. W.H. Freeman Spectrum, Oxford.

de Luce, J. & Wilder, H.T. (eds) (1983) *Language in Primates: Perspectives and Implications*. Springer-Verlag, New York.

Evans, C.S. (1997) Referential signals. *Perspectives in Ethology*, 12, 99–143.

Evans, C.S. & Marler, P. (1994) Food calling and audience effects in male chickens, *Gallus gallus:* their relationships to food availability, courtship and social facilitation. *Animal Behaviour*, 47, 1159–1170.

Ficken, M.S., Hailman, E.D. & Hailman, J.P. (1994) The chick-a-dee call system of the Mexican chickadee. *The Condor*, 96, 70–82.

Gardner, R.A., Gardner, B.T. & van Cantfort, T.E. (eds) (1989) *Teaching Sign Language to Chimpanzees*. State University of New York Press, Albany.

Gregory, R. & Hopkins, P. (1974) Pupils of a talking parrot. *Nature*, 252, 637–638.

Gyger, M. & Marler, P. (1988) Food calling in the domestic fowl, *Gallus gallus:* The role of external referents and deception. *Animal Behaviour*, 36, 358–365.

Herman, L.M., Pack, A.A. & Palmer, M-S. (1993) Representational and conceptual skills of dolphins. In H.L. Roitblat, L.M. Herman and P.E. Nachtigall, *Language and Communication: Comparative Perspectives*. Lawrence Erlbaum, New Jersey, pp. 403–442.

Hess, E.H. (1965) Attitude and pupil size. *Scientific American*, April 1965, 46–54.

Karakashian, S.J., Gyger, M. & Marler, P. (1988) Audience effects on alarm calling in chickens (*Gallus gallus*). *Journal of Comparative Psychology*, 102, 129–135.

Macedonia, J.M. & Evans, C.S. (1993) Variation among mammalian alarm call systems and the problem of meaning in animal signals. *Ethology*, 93, 177–197.

Marler, P. & Evans, C. (1996) Bird calls: just emotional displays or something more? *Ibis*, 138, 26–33.

Pepperberg, I. (1990a) Cognition in an African gray parrot (*Psittacus erithacus*): further evidence for comprehension of categories and labels. *Journal of Comparative Psychology*, 104, 41–52.

——(1990b) Some cognitive capacities of an African grey parrot (*Psittacus erithacus*). *Advances in the Study of Behavior*, 19, 357–409.

Premack, D. (1975) On the origins of language. In M.S. Gazzaniga & C. Blakemore (eds) *Handbook of Psychobiology*. Academic Press, New York, pp. 591–605.

Putney, R.T. (1985) Do wilful apes know what they are aiming at? *The Psychological Record*, 35, 49–62.

Rogers, L.J. (1997) *Minds of their Own: Thinking and Awareness in Animals*. Allen & Unwin, Sydney.

Roitblat, H.L., Herman, L.M. & Nachtigall, P.E. (eds) (1993) *Language and Communication: Comparative Perspectives*. Lawrence Erlbaum, New Jersey.

Rumbaugh, D. (1995) Primate language and cognition: common ground. *Social Research*, 62, 711–730.

Savage-Rumbaugh, S. & Lewin, R. (1994) *Kanzi: The Ape at the Brink of the Human Mind*. John Wiley & Sons, New York.

Sebeok, T.A. & Umiker-Sebeok, J. (eds) (1980) *Speaking of Apes: A Critical Anthology of Two-way Communication with Man*. Plenum Press, New York.

Seyfarth, R.M., Cheney, D.L. & Marler, P. (1980) Vervet monkey alarm calls: semantic communication in a free-ranging primate. *Animal Behaviour*, 28, 1070–1094.

Slobodchikoff, C.N., Kiriazis, J., Fischer, C. & Creef, E. (1991) Semantic information distinguishing individual predators in the alarm calls of Gunnison's prairie dogs. *Animal Behaviour*, 42, 713–719.

Wickler, W. (1968) *Mimicry in Plants and Animals*. Weidenfeld & Nicolson, London.

Chapter Three   Communication in birds

Adret, P. (1997) Discrimination of video images by zebra finches (*Taeniopygia guttata*): direct evidence from song performance. *Journal of Comparative Psychology*, 111(2), 115–125.

Andrew, R.J. (1961) The displays given by passerines in courtship and reproductive fighting. A review. *Ibis*, 103, 549–579.

Blaich, C., Steury, K.R., Pettengill, P., Mahoney, K.T. & Guha, A. (1996) Temporal patterns of contact call interactions in paired and unpaired domestic zebra finches (*Taeniopygia guttata*). International Society for Comparative Psychology Meeting, Montreal.

Borgia, G. (1995) Complex male display and female choice in the spotted bowerbird: specialized functions for different bower decorations. *Animal Behaviour*, 49(5), 1291–1301.

Busnel, R.-G. (1977) Acoustic communication. In T.A. Sebeok (ed.) *How Animals Communicate*. Indiana University Press, Bloomington, pp. 233–252.

Catchpole, C.K. & Slater, P.J.B. (1995) *Bird Song. Biological Themes and Variations*. Cambridge University Press, Cambridge.

Crook, J.H. (1969) Function and ecological aspects of vocalisation in weaver birds. In R.A. Hinde (ed.) *Bird Vocalisations*. Cambridge University Press, Cambridge, pp. 265–289.

Cruickshank, A.J., Gautier, J.-P. & Chappuis, C. (1993) Vocal mimicry in wild African Grey Parrots *Psittacus erithacus*. *Ibis*, 135, 293–299.

Evans, C.S. (1997) Referential signals. *Perspectives in Ethology*, 12, 99–143.

Fernald, A. (1992) Human maternal vocalizations to infants as biologically relevant signals: An evolutionary perspective. In J.H. Barkow, L. Cosmides & J. Tooby (eds) *The Adapted Mind: Evolutionary Psychology and the Generation of Culture*. Oxford University Press, New York, pp. 391–428.

Friedman, H. (1955) The honey guides. *US National Museum Bulletin*, 208, 1–279.

Frings, H. & Frings, M. (1956) Auditory and visual mechanisms in food-finding behaviour of the herring gull. *Wilson Bulletin*, 67, 155–170.

Greenewalt, C. (1968) *Bird song—physiology and acoustics*. Smithonian Institute Press, Washington.

Kirn, J.R., Clower, R.P., Kroodsma, D.E. & De Voogd, T.J. (1989) Song-related brain regions in the red-winged blackbird are affected by sex and season but not repertoire size. *Journal of Neurobiology*, 20, 139–163.

Kluender, K.R., Diehl, R.L. et al. (1987) Japanese quail can learn phonetic categories. *Science*, (Sept.), 1195–1197.

Kroodsma, D.E. (1996) Ecology of passerine song development. In D.E. Kroodsma and E.H. Miller (eds), *Ecology and Evolution of Acoustic Communication in Birds*. Comstock Publishing (Cornell University Press), Ithaca and London, pp. 3–19.

Kroodsma, D.E. & Parker, L.D. (1977) Vocal virtuosity in the brown thrasher. *Auk*, 94, 783–784.

Lambrechts, M.M., Clemmons, J.R. & Hailman, J.P. (1993) Wing quivering of black-capped chickadees with nestlings: invitation or appeasement? *Animal Behaviour*, 46(2), 397–399.

Lehrman, D.S. (1965) Interaction between hormonal and external environments in the regulation of the reproductive cycle of the ring dove. In F.A. Beach (ed.) *Sex and Behaviour*. Wiley, New York.

Leslie, R.F. (1985) *Lorenzo the Magnificent. The Story of an Orphaned Blue Jay*. John Curley & Associates, South Yarmouth, Ma.

Lorenz, K. (1966) *King Solomon's Ring*. Methuen & Co., London.

Marler, P. (1955) Characteristics of some animal calls. *Nature*, 176, 6–8.

——(1968) Aggregation and dispersal: two functions in primate communication. In P.C. Jay (ed.) *Primates: Studies in Adaptation and Variability*. Holt, Rinehart & Winston, New York.

——(1981) Bird song: the acquisition of a learned motor skill. *Trends in Neuroscience*, 4, 88–94.

Marler, P. & Tamura, M. (1964) Culturally transmitted patterns of vocal behavior in sparrows. *Science*, 146(3650), 1483–1486.

Patterson, D.K. & Pepperberg, I.M. (1996) A comparative study of human and parrot phonation: Acoustic and articulatory correlates of vowels. *Journal of the Acoustical Society of America*, 96, 634–648.

Pepperberg, I. (1990a) Cognition in an African gray parrot (*Psittacus erithacus*): further evidence for comprehension of categories and labels. *Journal of Comparative Psychology*, 104, 41–52.

——(1990b) Some cognitive capacities of an African grey parrot (*Psittacus erithacus*). *Advances in the Study of Behaviour*, 19, 357–409.

Robinson, F. & Robinson, A. (1970) Regional variation in the visual and acoustic signals of the male musk duck (*Biziura lobata*). *CSIRO Wildlife Research*, 15, 73–78.

Robinson, F.N. & Curtis, H.S. (1996) The vocal displays of the lyrebirds (*Menuridae*). *Emu*, 96, 258–275.

Saetre, G.-P. & Slagsvold, T. (1992) Evidence of sex recognition from plumage colour by the pied flycatcher, *Ficedula hypoleuca*. *Animal Behaviour*, 44(2), 293–299.

Saito, N. & Maekawa, M. (1993) Birdsong: the interface with human language. *Brain and Development*, 15, 31–40.

Slater, P.J.B. (1989) Bird song learning: causes and consequences. *Ethology, Ecology and Evolution*, 1, 19–46.

Smith, W.J. (1977) *The Behavior of Communicating: An Ethological Approach*. Harvard University Press, Cambridge, Mass.

Suthers, R.A. (1990) Contributions to birdsong from the left and right sides of the intact syrinx. *Nature*, 347, 473–477.

Thorpe, W.H. & Griffin, D.R. (1962) Lack of ultrasonic components in the flight noise of owls. *Nature*, 193, 594–595.

Tinbergen, N. (1953) *Social Behaviour in Animals*. Methuen, London.

Watanabe, S. (1993) Visual and auditory cues in conspecific discrimination learning in Bengalese finches. *Journal of Ethology*, 11, 111–116.

Williams, J.M. & Slater, P.J.B. (1990) Modelling bird song dialects: the influence of repertoire size and numbers of neighbours. *Journal of Theoretical Biology*, 145, 487–496.

Chapter Four Communication in mammals

Altringham, J.D. (1996) *Bats. Biology and Behaviour*. Oxford University Press, Oxford.

Andrew, R.J. (1972) The information potentially available in mammal displays. In R.A. Hinde (ed.) *Non-verbal communication*. Cambridge University Press, Cambridge.

Barrett-Lennard, L.G., Ford, J.K.B. & Heise, K.A. (1996) The mixed blessing of echolocation: differences in sonar use by fish-eating and mammal-eating killer whales. *Animal Behaviour*, 51(3), 553–565.

Boinski, S. (1991) The coordination of spatial position: a field study of the vocal behaviour of adult female squirrel monkeys. *Animal Behaviour*, 41(1), 89–102.

Brown, C., Gomez, R. et al. (1995) Old World monkey vocalizations: adaptation to the local habitat? *Animal Behaviour*, 50(4), 945–961.

Caldwell, M.C. & Caldwell, D.K. (1965) Individualized whistle contours in bottlenosed dolphins (*Tursiops truncatus*). *Nature*, 207, 434–435.

Chevalier-Skolnikoff, S. (1973) Facial expression of emotion in nonhuman primates. In P. Ekman (ed.) *Darwin and Facial Expression*. Academic Press, New York, pp. 11–90.

Cohen, S. (1994) *The Intelligence of Dogs. Canine Consciousness and Capabilities*. Free Press/Macmillan, Toronto.

Ekman, P. (ed.) (1974) *Darwin and Facial Expression*. Academic Press, New York.

Epple, G. (1968) *Folia Primatologica*, 8, 1–40.

——(1975) The behavior of marmoset monkeys (*Callithricidae*). In L.A. Rosenblum (ed.) *Primate Behavior. Developments in Field and Laboratory Research*. Academic Press, New York, pp. 195–239.

Epple, G., Küderling, I. et al. (1988) Some communicatory functions of scent marking in the cotton-top tamarin (*Saguinus oedipus oedipus*). *Journal of Chemical Ecology*, 14(2), 503–515.

Fadem, B.H. (1985) Chemical communication in gray short-tailed opossums (*Monodelphis domestica*) with comparisons to other marsupials and with reference to monotremes. In D. Duvall, D. Müller-Schwarze & R.M. Silberstein (eds) *Chemical Signals in Vertebrates. Vol. 4 Ecology, Evolution, and Comparative Biology*. Plenum Press, New York, pp. 587–607.

Fenton, M.B. (1994) Assessing signal variability and reliability: 'to thine ownself be true'. *Animal Behaviour*, 47(4), 757–764.

Fox, M.W. (1971) *Behaviour of Wolves, Dogs and Related Canids*. Jonathan Cape, London.

Fridlund, A.J. (1994) *Human Facial Expression. An Evolutionary View*. Academic Press, San Diego.

Gautier, J.-P. & Gautier, A. (1977) Communication in Old World monkeys. In T.A. Sebeok (ed.) *How Animals Communicate*. Indiana University Press, Bloomington, pp. 890–964.

Hanggi, E.B. & Schusterman, R.J. (1994) Underwater acoustic displays and individual variation in male harbour seals, *Phoca vitulina*. *Animal Behaviour*, 48(6), 1275–1283.

Hare, J.F. (1998) Juvenile Richardson's ground squirrels, *Spermophilus richardsonii*, discriminate among individual alarm callers. *Animal Behaviour*, 55, 451–460.

Hauser, M.D. (1993) Right hemisphere dominance for the production of facial expression in monkeys. *Science*, 261(23 July), 475–477.

Hauser, M.D., Teixidor, P. et al. (1993) Food-elicited calls in chimpanzees: effects of food quantity and divisibility. *Animal Behaviour*, 45(4), 817–819.

Hudson, R. & Vodermayer, T. (1992) Spontaneous and odour-induced chin marking in domestic female rabbits. *Animal Behaviour*, 43(2), 329–336.

Hurst, J.L., Fang, J. et al. (1993) The role of substrate odours in maintaining social tolerance between male house mice, *Mus musculus domesticus*. *Animal Behaviour*, 45(5), 997–1006.

Janik, V.M., Dehnhardt, G. & Todt, D. (1994) Signature whistle variations in a bottlenosed dolphin, *Tursiops truncatus*. *Behavioural Ecology and Sociobiology*, 35, 243–248.

Johnston, R.E. & Jernigan, P. (1994) Golden hamsters recognize individuals, not just individual scents. *Animal Behaviour*, 48(1), 129–136.

Johnston, R.E., Munver, R. & Tung, C. (1995) Scent counter marks: selective memory for the top scent by golden hamsters. *Animal Behaviour*, 49(6), 1435–1442.

Kaplan, G. & Rogers, L.J. (1994) *Orang-utans in Borneo*. University of New England Press, Armidale.

——(1996) *Gaze direction and visual attention in orang-utans*. XVI Congress of the International Primatological Society, Madison, Wisconsin.

Kellogg, W.N. (1961) *Porpoises and Sonar*. University of Chicago Press, Chicago.

Lewin, R. (1991) Look who's talking now. Do apes hold the key to the origin of human language? Ape-language studies with one chimpanzee suggest they just might. *New Scientist*, (27 April), 39–42.

McComb, K.E. (1991) Female choice for high roaring rates in red deer, *Cervus elaphus*. *Animal Behaviour*, 41(1), 79–88.

McCracken, G.F. (1993) Locational memory and female-pup reunions in Mexican free-tailed bat maternity colonies. *Animal Behaviour*, 45(4), 811–813.

MacKinnon, J. (1974) *In Search of the Red Ape.* William Collins, London.

Marler, P. (1968) Aggregation and dispersal: two functions in primate communication. In P.C. Jay (ed.) *Primates: Studies in Adaptation and Variability.* Holt, Rinehart & Winston, New York, pp. 420–438.

Marler, P. & Tenaza, R. (1977) Signaling behavior of apes with special reference to vocalizations. In T.A. Sebeok (ed.) *How Animals Communicate.* Indiana University Press, Bloomington, pp. 965–1033.

Newman, J.D. (1985) Squirrel monkey communication. In L.A. Rosenblum & C.L. Coe (eds) *Handbook of Squirrel Monkey Research.* Plenum Press, New York, pp. 99–126.

O'Connell, S. & Cowlishaw, G. (1994) Infanticide avoidance, sperm competition and mate choice: the function of copulation calls in female baboons. *Animal Behaviour,* 48(3), 687–694.

Payne, R. (1995) *Among Whales.* Scribner, London.

Preuschoft, S. (1992) Laughter and 'smile' in Barbary macaques (*Macaca sylvanus*). *Ethology,* 91, 220–236.

Provine, R.R. (1996a) Laughter. The study of laughter provides a novel approach to the mechanisms and evolution of vocal production, perception and social behavior. *American Scientist,* 84 (January/February), 38–45.

——(1996b) Contagious yawning and laughter: significance for sensory feature detection, motor patterns generation, imitation, and the evolution of social behavior. In C.M. Heyes & B.G. Galef (eds) *Social Learning in Animals: The Roots of Culture.* Academic Press, London, pp. 179–208.

Randall, J.A. (1994) Discrimination of foot-drumming signatures by kangaroo rats, *Dipodomys spectabilis. Animal Behaviour,* 47(1), 45–54.

Rendall, D., Rodman, P.S. & Edmond, R.E. (1996) Vocal recognition of individuals and kin in free-ranging rhesus monkeys. *Animal Behaviour,* 51(5), 1007–1015.

Schaller, G.B. (1963) *The Mountain Gorilla.* University of Chicago Press, Chicago.

Schrader, L. & Todt, D. (1993) Contact call parameters covary with social context in common marmosets, *Callithrix j. jacchus. Animal Behaviour,* 46(5), 1026–1028.

Stebbins, W.C. (1983) *The Acoustic Sense of Animals*. Harvard University Press, Cambridge, Mass.

Stoddart, D.M., Bradley, A.J. & Hynes, K.L. (1992) Olfactory biology of the marsupial sugar glider—a preliminary study. In R.L. Doty & D. Miller-Schwarze (eds) *Chemical Signals in Vertebrates Vol. 6*. Plenum Press, New York, pp. 523–528.

Todt, D., Goedeking, P. et al. (eds) (1988) *Primate Vocal Communication*. Springer, Berlin.

van Hooff, J.A. (1967) The facial expressions of the catarrhine monkeys and apes. In D. Morris (ed.) *Primate Ethology*. Weidenfeld & Nicolson, London.

Waal, F. de & Lanting, F. (1997) *Bonobo. The Forgotten Ape*. University of California Press, Berkeley.

Waser, P.M. & Waser, M.S. (1977) Experimental studies of primate vocalization: specializations for long-distance propagation. *Zeitschrift für Tierpsychologie*, 43, 239–263.

West, M.J., King, A.P. & Freeburg, T.M. (1997) Building a social agenda for the study of bird song. In C.T. Snowdon & M. Hausberger (eds) *Social Influences on Vocal Development*. Cambridge University Press, Cambridge, pp. 41–56.

Yamagiwa, J. (1992) Functional analysis of social staring behavior in an all-male group of mountain gorillas. *Primates*, 33(4), 523–544.

Chapter Five   Learning to communicate

Adret, P. (1993) Operant conditioning, song learning and imprinting to taped song in the zebra finch. *Animal Behaviour*, 46, 149–159.

Biben, M. & Bernhards, D. (1995) Vocal ontogeny of the squirrel monkey, *Saimiri boliviensis peruviensis*. In E. Zimmermen, J.D. Newman & U. Jürgens (eds) *Current Topics in Primate Vocal Communication*. Plenum Press, New York, pp. 99–140.

Curtiss, S., Fromkin, V., Krashen, S., Rigler, D. & Rigler, M. (1974) The linguistic development of Genie. *Language*, 50, 528–554.

Elowson, A.M. & Snowdon, C.T. (1994) Pygmy marmosets, *Cebuella pygmaea*, modify vocal structure in response to changed social environment. *Animal Behaviour*, 47, 1267–1277.

Farabaugh, S.M., Linzenbold, A. & Dooling, R.J. (1994) Vocal plasticity in budgerigars (*Melopsittacus undulatus*): evidence for social factors in the learning of contact calls. *Journal of Comparative Psychology*, 108, 81–92.

Fouts, R.S., Fouts, D.H. & van Cantfort, T.E. (1989) The infant Loulis learns signs from cross-fostered chimpanzees. In R.A. Gardner, B.T. Gardner & T.E. van Cantfort, *Teaching Sign Language to Chimpanzees*. State University of New York Press, Albany, pp. 280–292.

Gardner, R.A., Chiarelli, A.B., Gardner, B.T. & Plooij, F.X. (eds) (1994) *The Ethological Roots of Culture*. Kluwer Academic Press, Norwell, MA.

Green, S. (1975) Dialects in Japanese monkeys: vocal learning and cultural transmission of locale-specific vocal behaviour. *Zeitschrift für Tierpsychologie*, 38, 304–314.

Hauser, M.D. (1988) How infant vervet monkeys learn to recognise starling alarm calls: the role of experience. *Behaviour*, 105, 187–201.

——(1989) Ontogenetic changes in the comprehension and production of vervet monkey (*Cercopithecus aethiops*) vocalisations. *Journal of Comparative Psychology*, 103, 149–158.

Hauser, M.D. & Andersson, K. (1994) Left hemisphere dominance for processing vocalizations in adult, but not infant, rhesus monkeys: Field experiments. *Proceedings of the National Academy of Sciences*, USA, 91, 3946–3948.

Hinde, R.A. (ed.) (1969) *Bird Vocalizations: Their Relations to Current Problems in Biology and Psychology*. Cambridge University Press, Cambridge.

Hodun, A., Snowdon, C.T. & Soini, P. (1981) Subspecific variation in the long calls of the tamarin, *Saguinus fuscicollis*. *Zeitschrift für Tierpsychologie*, 57, 97–110.

Janik, V.M. & Slater, P.J.B. (1997) Vocal learning in mammals. *Advances in the Study of Behavior*, 26, 59–99.

Kaplan, G. & Rogers, L.J. (1994) *Orang-utans in Borneo*. University of New England Press, Armidale.

Kroodsma, D.E. (1978) Aspects of learning in the ontogeny of bird song. In G.M. Burghardt & M. Bekoff (eds) *The development of Behavior: Comparative and Evolutionary Aspects*. Garland, New York, pp. 215–230.

Le Boeuf, B. & Peterson, R.S. (1969) Dialects in elephant seals. *Science*, 166, 1654–1656.

Lehtonen, L. (1983) The changing song patterns of the great tit, *Parus major. Ornis Fennica,* 60, 16–21.

Lieblich, A.K., Symmes, D., Newman, J.D. & Shapiro, M. (1980) Development of the isolation peep in laboratory-bred squirrel monkeys. *Animal Behaviour,* 28, 1–9.

Lilly, J.C. (1965) Vocal mimicry in *Tursiops*: ability to match numbers and durations of human vocal bursts. *Science,* 147, 300–301.

Mann, N.I. & Slater, P.J.B. (1994) What causes young male zebra finches, *Taeniopygia guttata,* to choose their father as song tutor? *Animal Behaviour,* 47, 671–677.

Marler, P. (1970) Bird song and speech development: Could there be parallels? *American Science,* 58, 669–673.

——(1991) Differences in behavioural development in closely related species: birdsong. In P. Bateson (ed.) *The Development and Integration of Behaviour.* Cambridge University Press, Cambridge, pp. 41–70.

——(1997) Three models of song learning: Evidence from behaviour. *Journal of Neurobiology,* 33, 501–516.

Mitani, J.C. & Brandt, K.L. (1994) Social factors influence the acoustic variability in the long-distance calls of male chimpanzees. *Ethology,* 96, 233–252.

Morrice, M.G., Burton, H.R. & Green, K. (1994) Microgeographic variation and songs in the underwater vocalization repertoire of the Weddell seal (*Leptonychotes weddellii*) from the Vestfold Hills, Antarctica. *Polar Biology,* 14, 441–446.

Newman, J.D. (1995) Vocal ontogeny in macaques and marmosets: convergent and divergent lines of development. In E. Zimmermen, J.D. Newman & U. Jürgens (eds) *Current Topics in Primate Vocal Communication.* Plenum Press, New York, pp. 73-97.

Newman, J.D. & Symmes, D. (1982) Inheritance and experience in the acquisition of primate acoustic behavior. In C.T. Snowdon, C.H. Brown & M.R. Petersen (eds) *Primate Communication,* Cambridge University Press, Cambridge, pp. 259–278.

Nottebohm, F. (1989) From bird song to neurogenesis. *Scientific American,* Feb., 55–61.

Pepperberg, I.M., Brese, K.J. & Harris, B.J. (1991) Solitary sound play during acquisition of English vocalisations by an African Grey parrot (*Psittacus erithacus*): possible parallels with children's monologue speech. *Applied Psycholinguistics*, 12, 1151–1178.

Petitto, L.A. & Marentette, P.F. (1991) Babbling in the manual mode: Evidence for the ontogeny of language. *Science*, 251, 1493–1496.

Ralls, K., Fiorelli, P. & Gish, S. (1985) Vocalizations and vocal mimicry in captive harbor seals, *Phoca vitulina*. *Canadian Journal of Zoology*, 63, 1050–1056.

Reiss, D. & McCowan, B.M. (1993) Spontaneous vocal mimicry and production by bottlenose dolphins (*Tursiops truncatus*): evidence for vocal learning. *Journal of Comparative Psychology*, 107, 301–312.

Rogers, L.J. (1997) Early experiential effects on laterality: research on chicks has relevance to other species. *Laterality*, 2, 199–219.

Scott, J.P. & Fuller, J.L. (1965) *Genetics and the Social Behavior of the Dog*. University of Chicago Press, Chicago.

Seyfarth, R.L. & Cheney, D.M. (1986) Vocal development in vervet monkeys. *Animal Behaviour*, 34, 1640–1658.

Slater, P.J.B. (1986) The cultural transmission of bird song. *Trends in Ecology and Evolution*, 1, 94–97.

——(1989) Bird song learning: causes and consequences. *Ethology, Ecology and Evolution*, 1, 19–46.

Slater, P.J.B. & Ince, S.A. (1979) Cultural evolution in chaffinch song. *Behaviour*, 71, 146–166.

Slater, P.J.B. & Jones, A.E. (1997) Lessons in bird song. *Biologist*, 44, 301–303.

Slater, P.J.B., Ince, S.A. & Colgan, P.W. (1980) Chaffinch song types: their frequencies in the population and distribution between the repertoires of different individuals. *Behaviour*, 75, 207–218.

Smith, G.T., Brenowitz, E.A., Beecher, M.D. & Wingfield, J.C. (1997) Seasonal changes in testosterone, neural attributes of song control nuclei, and song structure in wild songbirds. *Journal of Neuroscience*, 17, 6001–6010.

Thorpe, W.H. (1961) *Bird Song*. Cambridge University Press, Cambridge.

Todt, D. (1975) Social learning of vocal patterns and modes of their application in grey parrots (*Psittacus erithacus*). *Zeitschrift für Tierpsychologie*, 39, 178–188.

Trainer, J.M. (1989) Cultural evolution in song dialects of yellow-rumped caciques in Panama. *Ethology*, 80, 190–204.

Weary, D. & Krebs, J. (1987) Birds learn song from aggressive tutors. *Nature*, 329, 485.

West, M.J. & King, A.P. (1988) Female visual displays affect the development of male song in the cowbird. *Nature*, 334, 244–246.

Zann, R. (1990) Song and call learning in wild zebra finches in south-east Australia. *Animal Behaviour*, 40, 811–828.

Chapter Six The evolution of communication

Andrew, R.J. (1956) Some remarks on behaviour in conflict situations, with special reference to *Emberiza* spp. *British Journal of Animal Behaviour*, 4, 41–45.

——(1965) The origins of facial expressions. *Scientific American*, October 1965, 88–94.

——(1972) The information potentially available in mammal displays. In R.A. Hinde (ed.) *Non-verbal Communication*. Cambridge University Press, Cambridge.

Bennett, A.T.D., Cuthill, I.C., Partridge, J.C. & Lunau, K. (1997) Ultraviolet plumage colors predict mate preferences in starlings. *Proceedings of the National Academy of Sciences, USA*, 94, 8618–8621.

Blakemore, C. & Cooper, G.F. (1970) Development of the brain depends on the visual environment. *Nature*, 228, 477–478.

Bradshaw, J.L. & Rogers, L.J. (1993) *The Evolution of Lateral Asymmetries, Language, Tool Use, and Intellect*. Academic Press, San Diego.

Catchpole, C.K. & Slater, P.J.B. (1995) *Bird Song: Biological Themes and Variations*. Cambridge University Press, Cambridge.

Dawkins, M.S. (1986) *Unravelling Animal Behaviour*. Longman, Harlow, UK. (Second edition 1995.)

Fitzgibbon, C.D. & Fanshaw, J.H. (1988) Stotting in Thomson's gazelles: an honest signal of condition. *Behavioral Ecology and Sociobiology*, 23, 69–74.

Guilford, T. & Dawkins, M.S. (1991) Receiver psychology and the evolution of animal signals. *Animal Behaviour*, 42, 1–14.

Hewes, G.W. (1973) Primate communication and the gestural origin of language. *Current Anthropology*, 14, 5–24.

Kuhl, P.K. (1988) Auditory perception and the evolution of speech. *Human Evolution*, 3, 19–43.

Lorenz, K. (1941) Vergleichende Bewegungsstudien an Anatiden. *Supplement of the Journal of Ornithology*, 89, 194–294.

——(1965) *Evolution and Modification of Behavior*. University of Chicago Press, Chicago.

McFarland, D. (1985) *Animal Behaviour: Psychobiology, Ethology and Evolution*. Pitman, London.

May, B., Moody, D.B. & Stebbins, W.C. (1989) Categorical perception of conspecific communication sounds by Japanese macaques, *Macaca fuscata*. *Journal of the Acoustic Society of America*, 85, 837–847.

Mollon, J.D. (1990) Uses and evolutionary origins of primate colour vision. In J.R. Cronly-Dillon and R.L. Gregory (eds) *Evolution of the Eye and Visual System*. Macmillan, pp. 306–319.

Morris, D. (1957) Typical intensity and its relation to the problem of ritualisation. *Behaviour*, 11, 1–12.

Neumeyer, C. (1990) The evolution of colour vision. In J.R. Cronly-Dillon & R.L. Gregory (eds) *Evolution of the Eye and Visual System*. Macmillan, pp. 284–305.

Petrie, M., Halliday, T. & Sanders, C. (1991) Peahens prefer peacocks with elaborate trains. *Animal Behaviour*, 41, 323–331.

Rogers, L.J. (1995) *The Development of Brain and Behaviour in the Chicken*. CAB International, Oxon.

Rogers, L.J. (1996) Behavioral, structural and neurochemical asymmetries in the avian brain: a model system for studying visual development and processing. *Neuroscience and Biobehavioral Reviews*, 20, 487–503.

Smith, W.J. (1977) *The Behavior of Communicating: An Ethological Approach*. Harvard University Press, Cambridge, Mass.

Tinbergen, N. (1960) *The Herring Gull's World*. Basic Books, NY.

——(1965) *The Study of Instinct*. Clarendon Press, Oxford.

Zahavi, A. (1979) Ritualisation and the evolution of movement signals. *Behaviour*, 72, 77–81.

Chapter Seven   Human–animal contacts

Arluke, A. (1994) Managing emotions in an animal shelter. In A. Manning & J. Serpell (eds) *Animals and Human Society: Changing Perspectives*. Routledge, London, pp. 145–165.

Blackshaw, J.K. (1996) Developments in the study of human–animal relationships. *Applied Animal Behaviour Science*, 47 (Special Issue: Human–Animal relationships), 1–6.

Candland, D.K. (1993) *Feral Children and Clever Animals: Reflections on Human Nature*. Oxford University Press, New York.

Clutton-Brock, J. (1994) The unnatural world. Behavioural aspects of humans and animals in the process of domestication. In A. Manning & J. Serpell (eds) *Animals and Human Society: Changing Perspectives*. Routledge, London, pp. 23–35.

Dawkins, M.S. (1993) *Through Our Eyes Only? The Search for Animal Consciousness*. Freeman Spektrum, Oxford.

Guttmann, G., Predovic, M. & Zemanek, M. (1985) The influence of pet ownership on non-verbal communication and social competence in children. In *Proceedings of International Symposium on Human-Pet Relationships*. IEMT, Vienna, 58–63.

Hart, L.A., Hart, B. & Bergin, B. (1987) Socializing effects of service dogs for people with disabilities. *Anthrozoös*, 1, 41.

Ingold, T. (1994) From trust to domination: an alternative history of human–animal relations. In A. Manning and J. Serpell (eds) *Animals and Human Society*. Routledge, London, pp. 1–22.

Kaplan, G. & Rogers, L.J. (1995) Of human fear and indifference: the plight of the orang-utan. In R.D. Nader, B. Galdikas, L. Sheehan & N. Rosen (eds) *The Neglected Ape*. Plenum Press, New York, pp. 3–12.

Kellert, S.R. (1994) Attitudes, knowledge and behaviour toward wildlife among the industrial superpowers—the United States, Japan and Germany. In A. Manning & J. Serpell (eds) *Animals and Human Society*. Routledge, London, pp. 166–187.

Levinson, B.M. (1969) *Pet-oriented Child Psychotherapy*. Charles C. Thomas, Springfield, Illinois.

Manning, A. & Serpell, J. (1994) *Animals and Human Society. Changing Perspectives*. Routledge, London.

Nelsen, A. (1987) *History of German Forestry: Implications for American Wildlife Management*. Yale School of Forestry and Environmental Studies, New Haven.

Newby, J. (1997) *The Pact for Survival. Humans and their Animal Companions*. Australian Broadcasting Corporation, Sydney.

Pinker, S. (1994) *The Language Instinct*. Penguin Books, London.

Roitblat, H.L., Harley, H.E. & Helwig, D.A. (1993) Cognitive processing in artificial language research. In H.L. Roitblat, L.M. Herman & P.E. Nachtigall (eds) *Language and Communication: Comparative Perspectives*. Lawrence Erlbaum, Hillsdale, NJ, pp. 1–23.

Serpell, J.A. (ed.) (1995) *The Domestic Dog. Its Evolution, Behaviour and Interactions with People.* Cambridge University Press, Cambridge.

Serpell, J.A. (1996) *In the Company of Animals. A Study of Human–Animal Relationships.* Cambridge University Press, Cambridge.

Settle, R.H., Sommerville, B.A. et al. (1994) Human scent matching using specially trained dogs. *Animal Behaviour,* 48(6), 1443–1448.

Snowdon, C.T. (1993) Linguistic phenomena in the natural communication of animals. In H.L. Roitblat, L.M. Herman & P.E. Nachtigall (eds) *Language and Communication: Comparative Perspectives.* Lawrence Erlbaum, Hillsdale, NJ, pp. 175–194.

Tudge, C. (1993) *The Engineer in the Garden. Genes and Genetics: From the Idea of Heredity to the Creation of Life.* Jonathan Cape, London.

INDEX

Bold refers to headings or subheadings;
italics refers to listings in the references